FRANCIS FAUGOIN

THE FORGOTTEN GARDENER OF STOURHEAD

FRANCIS FAUGOIN

JULIA MOTTERSHAW

Sponsored by Henry C Hoare

redcliffe

First published in 2023 by Redcliffe Press Ltd
81g Pembroke Road, Bristol BS8 3EA

info@redcliffepress.co.uk
www.redcliffepress.co.uk
Follow us on Twitter @RedcliffePress

ISBN 978-1-915670-09-0

Design and typesetting by Design Deluxe, Bath
Printed and Bound in the UK via Akcent Media Limited

FSC	MIX
www.fsc.org	Paper from responsible sources
	FSC® C014540

Redcliffe Press Ltd is committed to being an environmentally friendly publisher.
This book is made from Forest Stewardship Council® certified paper.

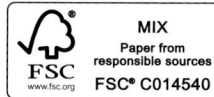

Front cover: Looking across the lake towards the Pantheon with autumn colours, at Stourhead, Wiltshire
© National Trust Images/Tony Gill

Frontispiece: View of the Pantheon across the lake at Stourhead, Wiltshire
© National Trust Images/Tamsin Holmes

CONTENTS

ACKNOWLEDGEMENTS

I COULD NOT have written this book without the help of friends and colleagues who have given their unstinting support and encouragement.

I would never have discovered so much about Francis Faugoin's family without the expert help of Jean Booth. Her skill in tracing family trees was invaluable. Whenever we hit a brick wall, she refused to give up. Lesser mortals would not have been so supportive and enthusiastic over such a long period of time.

Alan Power was Head Gardener at Stourhead for seventeen years. He was an inspiration and a patient mentor. Alan gave me the confidence to tell the story from my point of view.

Dudley Dodd took a keen interest in Francis from the beginning. I would not have been able to bring Henry the Magnificent to life without the help of his book *The Letters of Henry Hoare 1760–1781*. Dudley's meticulous attention to detail and careful referencing made my life much easier. My thanks also go to the Wiltshire Record Society who gave permission for me to quote from this publication.

Henry Cadogan Hoare believed that the story added new and valuable information to the existing history of Stourhead. His generous support and determination resulted in the publication of this book.

Being introduced to Crispin Powell, the archivist at Boughton, was a game-changer. He opened a treasure trove of information. He was delighted that I could bring to life a name that, to him, was just a name in the ledgers.

My good friends, Alan and Gillian Barker, acted as sounding boards as each chapter was written. Alan gave many hours of his time, using his expertise as a writer and editor to polish the text. Gillian came to the rescue when the flow of the narrative ground to a halt. She wisely and perceptively identified the problem and suggested a solution.

Anne Kaile shared my interest in garden history; our visits to Germany and Italy were memorable and fun. Anne is sharply observant and her dry sense of humour a delight.

At Stourhead, the National Trust staff and volunteers gave me their generous support and encouragement. My thanks also go to Philip Niemand, the General Manager, who helped to pave the way for this book to be published.

Pamela Hunter, archivist at C. Hoare & Co., introduced me to the Bank ledgers and found the letter from Francis Faugoin to Henry the Magnificent. Thanks to her, we had the pleasure of seeing Francis's handwriting and signature for the first time.

The archivists at the Wiltshire & Swindon History Centre could not have been more helpful. Special mention goes to Naomi Oakley whose experience and good humour calmed my nerves when deciding which Henry Hoare letter to include in the book.

My thanks also go to the staff at the Northamptonshire Record Office and the Hampshire Record Office who patiently took time to find the appropriate documents for me.

Clara Hudson and the team at Redcliffe Press Ltd worked tirelessly to transform this story into such a beautiful book.

My heartfelt thanks go to all of you.

JULIA MOTTERSHAW

FOREWORD

T IME AT STOURHEAD often stands still. One may simply be amazed by its beauty, mesmerised by the detail, or entirely captured by the overwhelming Spirit of the Place.

Time may stand still for most but there have always been those who engage with it on a deeper level – working in the shadow of the towering trees and monumental architecture, caring for it and ensuring its survival in a contemporary world. Throughout my twenty-four years at Stourhead, seventeen of them as Head Gardener, I met many people who were utterly captivated – enthralled by its beauty and fascinated by its history. However, there were a few whose passion, dedication and commitment went far beyond admiration and took them on a journey of discovery. Julia is one of them.

I delivered many tours of the garden, talks about its history and presentations about its conservation to staff and volunteers over the years, and Julia was at most of these events. Always there at the end, approaching politely with another question, to clarify a point, to arrange to pop into the office to chat further, and always with her notebook to hand. This is how it started: a fascination that led to hours, days, weeks and eventually years exploring the people who came together throughout history to create this magnificent work of art that we call Stourhead.

It was obvious to me when I met Julia that Stourhead would become more than just a place to her. I could see that she had the same hunger for it that I did and there is only one thing that will satisfy this hunger: to feed it with the great and intriguing stories of its past and then, most importantly – to share it. The joy of working with such intelligently created gardens is that there are always more stones to be turned and new discoveries to be made. Without people like Julia meticulously digging through the archives and records and sharing their findings, elements of these great narratives that help us to understand and interpret these wonderful places would surely be missed.

Julia's interest led her to study for a foundation degree in garden history and heritage horticulture, and this, in turn, helped to contextualise Stourhead and further anchor it as an iconic garden in terms of its moment of creation in the 18th century and subsequent evolution.

Never faltering on her journey to learn more, Julia continued to research and discover. But most importantly, she continued to share her findings, taking to the stage in front of friends, colleagues, and fellow historians. Her journey took her to where it all started – Hoare's Bank on Fleet Street, London. Here, she spoke to family members and staff and delved into the archives.

For Julia, Stourhead started as a masterpiece to wonder at. I can't imagine, following that first rainy day visit with her husband, that she could have foreseen it would become such a place of solace for her in the harder times, or that it would lead her on such an amazing journey of discovery.

Julia's work and passion over the years has led to this point. This is your opportunity to travel with her through the history of Stourhead: through its people, the family and their friends, and the gardeners. Some you will know, but others are new to most: notably, Francis Faugoin, a character of immense importance to the garden and to Henry Hoare II, the garden's creator.

During my time at Stourhead I read many, many books and documents about the place, the plants, and its history, each revealing yet another piece of the wonderful jigsaw. I just wish that this book had been sitting on my desk that day in 2003 when I arrived as Head Gardener, with a note simply saying – *'Read this first'*

ALAN POWER, NATIONAL TRUST GARDENS
AND PARKLANDS CONSULTANT

Faugoin graves | Photograph: the author

PROLOGUE

IT BEGAN WITH an ending. A name on a tomb: Francis Faugoin. The well-preserved lettering, still perfectly legible, revealed:

> In Memory of Francis Faugoin | who died 25th May 1788 | Aged 72 years
> Steward to the late Henry Hoare Esq. | with Whom he lived for 48 years

I came upon this imposing grave in the churchyard at the National Trust property at Stourhead, in Wiltshire. What surprised me more than anything else was the French-sounding name. I was a volunteer for the National Trust; I'd spent many years learning the history of this world-famous garden and the people who had created it. I'd taken hundreds of people on guided tours. And yet this name was completely new to me.

Francis Faugoin.

Who was he? Why was he remembered here? And buried in such a conspicuous part of the churchyard?

And why had I never heard of him?

Little did I think then that finding the answers to these questions would absorb, fascinate and frustrate me for several years, in the process of which I would make new friends, meet many interesting people and travel around the country and abroad.

What was I doing in the churchyard when I stumbled over this intriguing grave? I'd embarked on studying for a degree in garden history, and one of the assignments necessitated an exploration of the churchyard. But I'm moving ahead too quickly and need to retrace my steps and go back to the beginning.

My first-ever visit to Stourhead was such a disappointment. It poured with rain. Sitting in the car with my husband, I felt frustrated. I had come all this way just to see the trees and I did not intend to let the weather spoil my first glimpse of this famous, historic collection.

We were spending a few days' holiday with our daughter, Sarah, who lived only thirty minutes away. So, we decided to come back the next day, before returning home to Cheshire.

The next day dawned bright and clear. When we arrived, I was impatient to set off. Fortunately, we chose to head up the drive. I say 'fortunately' because it was only by chance that we took this route, rather than down to the lake, as most people do. Little did I know then that I would be taking this route hundreds of times in the future. Of course, the wonderful 600-year-old sweet chestnuts (*Castanea sativa*) along the drive were the first trees I'd come to see. Their great, bulky, twisted shapes commanded attention.

As the drive curved away in front of us, an impressive house came into view. I hadn't realised that there was a house; I knew nothing about its history or the people who had lived there. Not being especially interested in the house, we turned away and walked into the garden, passing a large Indian bean tree (*Catalpa bignonioides*), and out onto the spacious lawn behind the house.

I was simply astonished by the size of the trees. And what trees! A towering tulip tree (*Liriodendron tulipifera*), a coast redwood (*Sequoia sempervirens*) and a venerable old English oak (*Quercus robur*): how old were these trees? Who had planted them? I did know that the tulip tree was first introduced into this country by John Tradescant the Younger in 1688, after visiting the east coast of North America. I knew also that the first descriptions and drawings of the coast redwood from the west coast caused a sensation when news of their existence was reported. I could identify these trees, but there were so many others I hadn't seen before. I later recorded in my garden diary: 'Absolutely stunning trees, enormous Liriodendron. Wonderful panoramic views and vistas.' My interest in the trees stemmed from the fact that at the time I worked at Bridgemere, a large nursery and garden centre in Cheshire. I was a member of the plant advisory team and my colleagues had insisted that I see the Stourhead tree collection.

We followed the path, down a slope, and then – wow! – something I was not expecting.

It's almost impossible to describe that first, glorious view of the Temple of Apollo. We just stood and gazed. The ground fell sharply away in front of us, and we realised we were looking down into a valley. There seemed to be a river: we caught a glimpse of water and a bridge. Trees poured down the hillside in front of us, green upon green. A huge rhododendron teetered on the edge, leaning over precariously, the brilliant colour of the deep-pink flowers only intensifying the green. The ground rose steeply on the other side of the valley, clothed with more and more trees, and this temple nestled in their midst.

My excitement knew no bounds. What would we see next?

Even then, on that very first visit, Stourhead started to cast its spell over me. I would never have believed I was destined to stand on this spot many, many times in the future, and to talk about this view to visitors from all over the world.

Continuing down the winding path under the shade of the towering beeches, we looked to the left – and another unforgettable sight came into view: a classical building beside an expanse of water, framed by more trees. It appeared to hover or float above the water, its reflection shimmering in the sunshine. Trees blocked the view to the right and to the left, so that only this little cameo was visible. The view took our breath away. It seemed unreal, a dream. It was also disorientating: we couldn't work out this temple's location in relation to the first one. I did at least know that the building we could see resembled the Pantheon in Rome.

As we walked down the hillside, the path became steeper, giving more glimpses of water through the trees. As we rounded the corner, the whole glorious picture was revealed.

Now I understood. We saw a beautiful lake with the Pantheon on the far side, a bridge over the water and the Temple of Apollo (as I now know) perched high on the hillside to the left.

I began to realise that there was more to this garden than just the trees. Why was it here? Who made it? When? And why? So many questions I was unable to answer.

As we left, I spotted the guidebook and – hurray! – a tree list. At least I could read that on the way home.

If only I had not been so impatient when we arrived, I might have been better informed. On the other hand, I'd experienced the magic of Stourhead's design without any preconceptions: surprise, variety, concealment. I've witnessed visitors expressing the same surprise and enjoyment so many times, but I have never forgotten my own powerful first impression.

Two years later, we moved to Wiltshire.

Apollo view | Photograph: the author

Henry Hoare I
MICHAEL DAHL (1656–1743)
Oil painting on canvas | circa 1722 | © National Trust Images
In his right hand, Henry Hoare holds a partly unfurled scroll of plans for the façade of Stourhead.

CHAPTER ONE

THE BANKER

H AVING BECOME A volunteer for the National Trust at Stourhead, I began to learn its history.

I learnt that the creator of the Stourhead landscape garden, Henry Hoare II, was a banker in London in the middle of the 18th century. I learnt also that the bank, C. Hoare & Co., remains open for business to this day, the sole survivor of the private banks that were established in the 17th and 18th centuries in London. Henry's father was Henry Hoare I, known affectionately by the family as 'Good Henry', as a result of his many philanthropic deeds. Concerned about the lack of hospitals for the poor in London, Hoare and others funded the foundation of the Westminster Hospital, known today as the Chelsea and Westminster. Good Henry also proposed another radical idea, that medical care should be free, funded by means of contributions from charitable societies. He was a 'devout man with a social conscience and a practical nature'[1] and left money in his will to many other charities and good causes. He provided an exemplary role model for his son. Indeed, C. Hoare & Co continues to support many charities with the help of the Golden Bottle Trust.

Henry II was born in 1705, the third of Good Henry's five children with his wife, Jane. His two older sisters, Jane and Susanna, were three years and one year older respectively. His two younger siblings, Martha and Richard, were three and four years younger. The family lived at the banking premises at 37 Fleet Street, London, in rooms on the first floor, above the banking hall, referred to as 'the shop'. It must have been a crowded and noisy household, with five children under eight years old.

By the time Henry was born, the Hoares had established themselves as goldsmiths and bankers in London. Henry's grandfather, Richard, served his apprenticeship with the goldsmith Robert Tempest. Tempest had set up his business at the sign of the Golden Bottle in Goldsmiths Row, Cheapside. Richard began his apprenticeship in 1665, just as the Great Plague hit London. One year later, London suffered the Great Fire. It is something of a miracle that Richard not only survived these two cataclysmic events but went on to become a successful businessman. When Tempest died, Richard bought the business from his widow. On 5th July 1672, he became a Freeman of the Worshipful Company of Goldsmiths and so was permitted to trade under his own name. This date marked the beginning of Richard's career as a goldsmith.[2]

Richard's father, another Henry, came from a family of yeoman farmers, the term indicating that they owned the land on which they lived and farmed, and belonged to the social class just below the gentry. This Henry had come to London with his wife and set himself up in business as a horse trader. This was a respectable position, requiring sound knowledge and good judgement of horses – an essential skill at a time when horses were the only means of transport. He was honest and trustworthy; his standing in the community was recognised when he was elected as Overseer of the Poor, responsible for the distribution of poor relief in the parish. So, early on, the Hoares demonstrated a social conscience and a willingness to accept civic responsibility.

Goldsmiths were not only makers and dealers in gold and silver wares, but also bankers for their customers. Hoare's Bank customers could feel confident that their money and precious belongings were held in secure premises. The term 'banker' was rarely used on its own before 1700; men of business such as Richard Hoare were referred to as 'goldsmith-bankers'.[3] The goldsmith-banker took cash on deposit and issued a receipt. These receipts, known as goldsmith's notes, were payable on demand and circulated instead of coins. This was a new and innovative service being offered as an alternative to carrying cash, at a time when London was the largest city in Europe, rapidly developing its commercial trade with the rest of the world. Richard and his son Henry were pioneers in developing this side of the business, leaving goldsmithing behind and concentrating on banking.

In 1690, Richard moved premises from Cheapside to 37 Fleet Street, where the bank still conducts its business today. The Bank of England did not yet exist, being founded in 1694, so Richard had a head start of over twenty years in developing his business. He was knighted by Queen Anne in 1702 on the occasion of her coronation. 'That great goldsmith-banker, Sir Richard Hoare', as he was now known, became Lord Mayor of London in September 1712, when he was sixty-four years old. He had founded a banking dynasty.

It is not difficult to imagine the young Henry proudly looking on when his grandfather Richard, wearing all the regalia of Lord Mayor, passed along Fleet Street in the Lord Mayor's procession. He would have only been seven years old but those kinds of occasions, so splendid and exciting, must have stayed long in his memory. Maybe he began to realise, too, the importance of working hard and maintaining an income – and that being successful carried responsibilities. In a later letter to his nephew, he talked about 'what great things may be done by application to business'.

As he grew up, Henry attended Westminster School in London. There he met a fellow schoolboy, William Beckford, who was four years older and destined to become

a neighbour and friend. The future Alderman Beckford would buy the estate at Fonthill Gifford, a few miles from Stourhead, and build a mansion there. He too, like Richard Hoare, would be honoured with the post of Lord Mayor of London. Another schoolfriend, The Hon. Charles Hamilton, went on to inherit an estate and create a garden at Painshill in Surrey, which can still be visited today. Hamilton borrowed £6,568 from Hoare's Bank in 1766 to fund his gardening activities, which he paid back in full in July 1773.

When he left school, Henry was taken into the family business. He became a partner when he was only twenty, after the sudden death of his father, Good Henry. His Uncle Benjamin was also a partner; his younger brother, Richard, entered the partnership in 1731. One year later, a new partnership agreement was drawn up and Henry, at the age of twenty-seven, became Senior Partner, taking a half share of the profits.[4]

As a young man, Henry's favourite pursuits were horse racing and fox hunting. All his life, riding gave him enormous pleasure: the exercise alone must have been an antidote to the stresses and strains of running the bank, which he was to do for fifty-one years. His letters reveal this passion: 'I took a gallop on Miss Cade over the downs last week with Mr. Barton to Mr. Beckford's,' he wrote on one occasion. Montagu Barton was the vicar at Stourton. Miss Cade came from a famous line of thoroughbreds: her sire, Cade, was one of the founding line of the Godolphin Arabians. When it came to judging a good horse, I think Henry must have inherited his great-grandfather's genes.

By the age of twenty-one, Henry had married. His wife, Anne Masham, was eighteen, the daughter of Samuel, Lord Masham, and his wife Abigail. The Mashams were friends of Henry's grandfather, Sir Richard. Abigail had become the confidante of Queen Anne and was instrumental in bringing the Privy Purse account to Hoare's Bank.

Henry and Anne were married on 11th April 1726, a few months before his twenty-first birthday, and Anne brought with her an exceptional dowry of £10,000. The marriage was seen as a sound financial investment, and was no doubt viewed with satisfaction by Henry's father and grandfather. What Henry's feelings were, we do not know.

Just over a year later a daughter, Anne, was born. When the little girl was less than a year old, her mother died. She is buried at Stourton. Little Anne lived with her grandmother, Jane, at Stourhead when Henry remarried, but sadly died just before her ninth birthday.

Henry married again on 6th July 1728, the day before his twenty-third birthday. Susan Colt was twenty years old and the daughter of Stephen Colt, a successful businessman trading in Surat, India. She was born an heiress and the marriage settlement brought Henry a further £14,000. They were to have five children: three boys and two girls. Susan died in 1743, when she was only thirty-five, after fifteen years of what appeared to be a successful marriage.

Henry never married again.

He was now thirty-eight and a widower twice over. He had been catapulted into the serious responsibilities of banking at an early age; he had enjoyed all the usual pursuits of the wealthy young men of his day; and he had a family. But there was no sign as yet of the passions and skills that would make him famous in the years to come.

---

1 Hutchings, Victoria. *Messrs. Hoare Bankers.*
   A History of the Hoare Banking Dynasty.
   Constable & Robinson Ltd, London, 2005. p. 39.

2 Ibid. p. 10.

3 Ibid. p. 11.

4 Ibid. p. 49.

CHAPTER TWO
THE GARDENER

T HE ACCIDENTAL DISCOVERY of this intriguing tomb presented many questions, not least 'Who was this man?'

I thought the best plan of action initially was to try to understand the layout of the churchyard and the meaning of the symbols on the headstones. I asked Alan Power for advice. Alan was Stourhead's Head Gardener at the time and was always most willing to share his extensive knowledge. He was full of enthusiasm; it was always a joy talking to him. He immediately suggested his ex-wife Sonja, who also worked for the Trust and was an expert on such matters. Sonja, said Alan, could tell the history of any headstone from fifty paces. Clearly she was the person I needed to see.

Sonja kindly offered to meet me in the churchyard. She explained that symbols were carved on the older headstones so that people who could not read were able to understand them. For instance, an urn was a popular symbol, which may have represented the soul. A skull and crossbones was a reminder to the onlooker that death comes to us all: a memento mori.

Close-up of grave | Photograph: the author

Sonja also told me that there was a strict hierarchy in the positioning of graves. People of high status were buried within the church, and those of a slightly lower status as close to the church as possible. Close to the church; closer to God. Since medieval times, graves of respectable people had not been placed on the north side of the church, where, it was thought, the devil resided. The area was reserved for criminals and the unbaptised.[1] This custom persisted until the 19th century.

I clambered up the hillside to look at more graves. It became apparent that the steepness of the site and difficulty of access did not deter people from wishing to be buried on the south side. Now I understood that the Faugoin tomb was in a significant and prominent position, close to the church and highly visible when approaching the entrance.

It is a large, limestone chest tomb with a flat top, typical of the period and Grade II listed. The well-preserved lettering, still perfectly legible, revealed:

> In Memory of Francis Faugoin | who died 25th May 1788 | Aged 72
> years | Steward to the late Henry Hoare Esq. | with Whom he lived for 48 years

alongside another inscription:

> Also Mary | wife of Francis Faugoin | who died Dec. 11th 1785 | Aged 68 years.

On closer inspection, I found other Faugoin family members buried close by: two boys, Felix and John; and a granddaughter of Felix. So, I now knew that this mystery person had a wife and family, and that he had worked for Henry Hoare II for many years.

By this point, of course, I knew that Henry Hoare II – 'Henry the Magnificent', as he became known – had created the garden at Stourhead in the second half of the 18th century. Now, astonishingly, it slowly dawned on me that Francis Faugoin had worked at Stourhead throughout that period. I then remembered reading in the 2014 guidebook the only reference to him, briefly stating:

> ... A team of 50 gardeners, supervised by Henry's steward Francis Faugoin,
> planted and tended beech, oak, sycamore ...[2]

The information that there were '50 gardeners' came from a visitor to the garden in 1776. The diarist and social commentator Mrs Lybbe Powys recorded:

> ... Fifty men are constantly employ'd in keeping the pleasure-grounds,
> rides & c. in order ...[3]

A lifetime of service meant that Francis must have begun working for Henry when he was a young man, presumably working his way up from Head Gardener to the important position of Steward (as inscribed on his tomb).

Obviously, his story had long been forgotten. After all, who will remember us in two hundred years?

I began to wonder: what was this man's role in the story of Stourhead? Famous gardens don't just happen. Behind the vision lies a huge amount of hard, down-to-earth, practical work – as any gardener will know. Indeed, the dedicated team caring for the garden today continue to look after the original vision, often asking the question, 'What would Henry have done?' Francis Faugoin must have been one of the many people who worked on the estate: the builders, gardeners, stonemasons ... But he must have had enough importance to warrant an imposing tomb in a prominent position. Why?

This idle thought propelled me, and others, on a journey of discovery that took several years. And there are still things we do not know about him, even now.

Just behind the Faugoin tomb, almost hidden, was a simple headstone lying flat on the ground on which was inscribed the words:

> In Memory of Jane Lloyd who died Jan 2nd 1807
> Aged 82 years Housekeeper to the late Henry Hoare Esq.
> And the present Rich'd Hoare Bt. With whom she lived 37 years.

The two old retainers, the gardener/steward and the housekeeper, were buried side by side.

The ancient church of St Peter's and its churchyard are in the small village of Stourton in Wiltshire, on the very edge of Stourhead itself. The 'ton' on the River Stour was a Saxon settlement, possibly a trading post using the river for transporting goods and people. The Stour rises nearby at the head of a valley and enters the sea at Christchurch. The first reference to a stone church on the site was in 1291,[4] when it may have replaced an earlier simple wooden building. It is also likely to have been built on an even earlier pagan site, where the spirits of the river were worshipped.

The church houses memorials to members of the Hoare family. An elaborate Baroque memorial to Henry Hoare I (Good Henry) was placed there by his wife, Jane, and lists his many philanthropic deeds and interests. A much simpler memorial to Henry Hoare II (Henry the Magnificent) details his family and includes a poem inscribed on a scroll. The memorial to Hester Hoare, the wife of Sir Richard Colt Hoare (Henry II's grandson), features a marble sarcophagus and two cherubs on either side of an urn.

The church and churchyard are an integral part of the Grade I historic English landscape garden that is Stourhead. They played an important part in the original design when Henry Hoare II first created the garden, or pleasure grounds as they were called. The view from the Pantheon across the lake to the Palladian bridge and the Bristol Cross, with the village and church in the background, was the vision which Henry had in his mind when creating his 'picture'. He may have been inspired, in part, by Gaspard Dughet, an artist he much admired. The picture gallery in the house contains two landscapes by Dughet. Henry wrote to his daughter Susanna in 1762:

> ... The View of the Bridge, Village and Church alltogether [sic] Will be a Charmg Gasp^d picture at the end of that Water.[5]

This view is perfectly captured in a painting by Henry's great friend, the artist Coplestone Warre Bampfylde (1720–1791). Unlike some of his contemporaries, Henry wanted to preserve the village community, with the 13th-century church nestling in its midst, and so he wished to include the church in his design. People were important to him.

The view looking the other way, from the church back across the lake to the Pantheon, is probably the best-known view of Stourhead. Bampfylde also painted this view, with figures in the foreground. Both these paintings are signed and dated. They are in black ink and watercolour, and today hang in the Library at Stourhead.

In the summer of 1833, J.C. Loudon (1783–1843), the influential garden writer of the early 19th century, visited Stourhead, saying:

> The church and churchyard are pleasingly situated on a sloping bank and the churchyard is one of the best kept which are to be seen in England. Roses and other flowering shrubs are planted against the church; Cypresses and other trees are sprinkled among the graves and the grass is kept as smooth as any lawn. The tombs of the Hoare family are in an open chapel at one end of the church and the tombs of their stewards at the other, the latter containing the remains of three generations of the same family.
>
> The fence is a sunk wall with its perpendicular side towards the church, so that at a short distance there appears to be no fence at all, and the whole seems a component part of the pleasure ground. We have seldom seen anything so well managed ...[6]

Loudon is describing what must obviously have been a ha-ha between the church and the garden, having the effect of making the church, churchyard and pleasure grounds merge into one.

I was surprised that Loudon chose to draw attention to the graves of the steward and his family. Over two hundred years later, I was also paying attention to these graves and beginning what would become, for me and others, a passion and obsession.

1 Calland, G. *St. Peter's, Stourton: A Tour and History of the Church.* Henry Cadogan Hoare, 2010. pp. 30–31.
2 Garnett, Oliver and Lambert, Anthony, eds. *Stourhead.* Park Lane Press, Corsham, for National Trust (Enterprises) Ltd, 2014. p. 17.
3 Climenson, Emily J., ed. *Passages from the Diaries of Mrs. Philip Lybbe Powys of Hardwick House, Oxon, 1756–1808.* Longmans, London, 1889.
4 Calland, G. *St. Peter's, Stourton: A Tour and History of the Church.* p. 12.
5 Dodd, Dudley, ed. *The Letters of Henry Hoare 1760–1781.* WSA 1300/4280. p. 42.
6 Boniface, P., ed. *In Search of English Gardens: The Travels of John Claudius Loudon and His Wife Jane.* Guild Publishing, 1987.

CHAPTER THREE
NEW OPPORTUNITIES

Y HUSBAND, IAN, and I had made the decision to move house so that we could see more of our three children, who had all migrated south from Cheshire. Christmas was fast approaching, and we needed some inspiration for presents. We thought the National Trust shop at Stourhead would give us some ideas. While looking round, my husband spotted a small card in the window asking for volunteers to work in the plant centre. He looked at me and said, "You could do that".

This made me smile. The 'plant centre' at Stourhead was tiny.

In Cheshire, I'd worked at Bridgemere Nurseries, a large garden centre, owned by a well-respected horticulturalist, John Ravenscroft. Bridgemere was rather unusual: not only were many of the plants propagated and grown on the forty-acre site, but it also had rose fields, a tree yard and a five-acre show garden. It employed a dedicated, knowledgeable team who advised customers about anything and everything to do with plants. I was a member of this team; we were based in a small conservatory on the site. There were always queues of people waiting to talk about which variety of apple tree to choose for a small garden, or which was the best evergreen hedging. They would bring along leaves for identification. They would ask, "Can you prune a magnolia?" or "What pest or disease is attacking my plum tree?" The list of questions was endless. My boss, Nigel Snow, was a 'tree man'. He'd even planned his honeymoon around a trip to America to see the coast redwoods in their natural habitat.

While I was working at Bridgemere, I attended evening lectures given by the garden centre's Production Manager, Chris Sanders. Chris was also a lecturer at Keele University. He had an encyclopaedic knowledge, was a member of the Woody Plants Committee at Wisley, and had led many plant-hunting expeditions to China and the Himalayas. His photographs of these landscapes were exceptional – beautiful and memorable – and they included detailed close-ups of the wild flowers and plants.

These two people, Nigel and Chris, taught me to look at plants and trees: to really look, look, and look again at every small detail. I learnt to observe the shape of leaves, their colour and texture (both front and back), their position on the stem – alternate or opposite – and, of course, the Latin names.

I was inspired to sign up for the Royal Horticultural Society's three-year course – the RHS General Studies. On the first day, I met Carolyn Estcourt, a passionate plantswoman. We subsequently worked together at Bridgemere and made many friends. I still seek her advice when I need help identifying a plant. I also keep in touch with Babs Hilton, who took me under her wing when I joined the team. Babs was a good teacher and good fun.

Missing Bridgemere, I decided to apply for the position at the Stourhead plant centre. I was delighted to be accepted: now I could be back among plants and people. Of course, it also meant that I became a volunteer for the National Trust.

A year later, the Trust launched a new initiative. It planned to offer free guided tours to the public to tell the story of Stourhead: who made it, why and when. The tours were to be called Walks and Talks, and I joined a small team of six guides. I now had a lot to learn, and fast. Luckily, a new book by Tim Richardson had just been published called *The Arcadian Friends*.[1] Reading this book introduced me to the concept of garden history. The author was described as a 'garden historian', a term that intrigued me. What a wonderful thing to do, I thought: to combine history and gardening.

I had always loved history, but until now my main interest had been the Anglo-Saxons and the foundation of the English nation under Alfred the Great and his grandson, Athelstan. I remember, as we moved south from Cheshire, being thrilled at the thought of living in Wessex, where Alfred fought and defeated the Danes at the historic battle of Ethandun in 878. The site of this battle is believed to be close to the village of Edington, which has a statue of Alfred in the centre.

Now I plunged into the 18th century in general, and the English Landscape Movement in particular. It was all new territory to me. Stourhead proved to be the perfect environment, combining history and gardens. What could be better than that? It was as if a door had been opened a tiny crack, and I could just see (in the words of Howard Carter, the discoverer of Tutankhamen's tomb) 'wonderful things'.

The Walks & Talks tours proved to be very popular and the team was soon expanded to twelve guides. I was beginning to understand what it meant to work in a world-famous historic garden. I learnt more about the Hoare banking family, who bought the Stourton estate in 1717, built the Palladian mansion and created the landscape garden, their descendants living there until bequeathing it to the National Trust in 1946. There was so much to learn.

A turning point came when I spotted a small advertisement in *The Garden*, the monthly magazine of the Royal Horticultural Society. It asked for applications for a new course being offered by the University of the West of England: a degree in garden history and heritage horticulture. I couldn't believe my luck on reading that the classes would be held at Hestercombe, near Taunton, which was only an hour from where I lived.

With my husband's encouragement and some trepidation, I decided to apply. To my great delight, I was accepted.

The lectures took place once a week for three years. Hestercombe is today mainly known for its garden, designed by Gertrude Jekyll and Edwin Lutyens; but there is an older, 18th-century garden, stretching up the combe behind the house, with many similar features to Stourhead. I'd never been to Hestercombe and only later discovered that the creator of this garden, Coplestone Warre Bampfylde, was a contemporary and close friend of Henry the Magnificent. I didn't realise how important this place would be to my story, and to the story of Stourhead.

I well remember the first day when, as is the usual format, everyone went round the room introducing themselves, giving a brief account of what they did. I was surprised to learn that another student, Anne Kaile, introduced herself as a volunteer at Stourhead, working as a member of the garden team as a hands-on gardener. We'd never met; working in different teams and probably on different days, our paths had never crossed. Stourhead is a big place with over four hundred volunteers, so it's entirely possible that we would never have met if not for joining this course.

Anne and I became good friends. We have had many garden history adventures together, and we still do.

The next three years were an eye-opener. The course covered the history of gardening from the Egyptians to the present day, taking in Islamic gardens, Italian Renaissance gardens, the English Landscape Movement, Victorian kitchen gardens and 20th-century designers along the way. It also included an in-depth study of plants, conservation and ecology. It was stimulating, hard work, sometimes stressful but hugely enjoyable.

One aspect of this course proved to be a steep learning curve. The subject matter was well within my comfort zone, I was well qualified in horticulture, and history had always been a favourite subject, but it was apparent that most people were more computer literate than I was. I could use a computer at a basic level but had never been tasked with producing a significant amount of work.

I've never forgotten coming home feeling deeply despondent and saying, "I don't think I can do this," and my husband asking, "Why?". When I told him the problem, he looked at me in disbelief and some amusement and said, "You are definitely going to do this; you're made for it," which bolstered my confidence. Ian was always a great believer in encouraging people to take on challenges and stretch themselves. I'd very nearly given up before I'd even started, but my husband was adamant that I would master this skill.

One of the assignments was to produce a Conservation Management Plan (or CMP). I chose the churchyard at Stourhead as my subject. My tutor thought this was rather a strange choice, but I persuaded him of its merits. The churchyard represents an important element in the design concept of the garden; at that time, the grounds were managed by the National Trust, who were keen to emphasise the environmental aspects of an ancient churchyard. Today, many National Trust properties have detailed and expensive Conservation Management Plans, but Stourhead was the first to produce such a plan, in 1978.[2] The aim of the plan was to 'formulate a series of principles ... that would reconcile the successive changes in a way that reveals and emphasises the original intention, while retaining and gradually adjusting many of the subsequent developments'. These 'subsequent developments' referred to the many changes introduced by members of the Hoare family down the years, as well as changes introduced by the National Trust, necessary for managing an ever-increasing number of visitors. In his book *Shades of Green*,[3] John Sales says, 'It takes a masterpiece of supreme strength and resilience to absorb two and a half centuries of development and go on to give ever more pleasure and spiritual refreshment to so many.'

The team put together to produce this document must have done a good job. Their CMP remains relevant today. Alan Power always referred to it as his 'bible'. Clearly, my feeble efforts at producing a CMP did not begin to approach the complexity of the real thing. Nonetheless, I had to demonstrate an awareness and understanding of the main principles involved, hence my exploration of the churchyard.

Although I found this assignment quite difficult, I'm eternally grateful to my tutor for going along with my suggestion of using the churchyard as the subject matter. It meant that I had to carefully examine all aspects: topography, history, location, its place in the overall design of the garden, and, of course, the people who were buried there.

If I had not chosen this place, at this time, I would never have noticed the tomb of Francis Faugoin. The questions I asked would lead to the discovery of an extraordinary story: the story of an ordinary man who lived and worked at Stourhead, took part in its creation, and ultimately became Henry the Magnificent's right-hand man. Francis Faugoin had been hiding in plain sight for over two hundred years. Serendipity led me to discover his story.

I turned to a friend and fellow volunteer for help, Jean Booth. Jean and I had worked together previously, when uncovering the story of another occupant of the churchyard, Thomas Hurle and his family. Jean was just as keen as me to learn more about Francis Faugoin; she was also a skilled genealogist. She had years of experience of investigating family histories, including her own. She was a dab hand at creating a family tree, as if by magic, it seemed to me.

Jean was equally intrigued by the inscription on the tomb and set about seeing what she could find. It didn't take her long to find a marriage record for Francis, which confirmed that he and Mary Swetman had married at the church of St Mary Magdalene, Old Fish Street, London, on 16th January 1739, when Francis was twenty-three years old. Even better, the record revealed that he was a bachelor of Grateley, Hampshire and she was a spinster of St Giles in the Fields, London.

Now we could trace Francis to Grateley in Hampshire – or so we hoped.

The hunt was on.

1 Richardson, Tim. *The Arcadian Friends: Inventing the English Landscape Garden*. Bantam Press, 2007.

2 *The Conservation of the Garden at Stourhead and Parts of the Park relating to it: Report and Recommendations of the Committee appointed by the National Trust*. Bath University Press, for the National Trust, 1978.

3 Sales, John. *Shades of Green. My Life as the National Trust's Head of Gardens*. Unicorn Publishing Group LLP, London, 2018.

CHAPTER FOUR

THE GRATELEY/
QUARLEY
CONNECTION

G OOD HENRY HOARE bought the Manor of Stourton and old Stourton House
for £14,250 in 1717, one year before the death of his father, Sir Richard. Together
they had planned to invest in land and property in the countryside, not too far from
London. Henry's attention had turned to Wiltshire.

He knew the area because his brother-in-law, William Benson, had built a small,
single-storey Palladian house at Newton Tony near Amesbury in 1710, which he
named Wilbury.

William Benson was perceived by many of his contemporaries as a vainglorious
opportunist. He had travelled on the Continent and admired the classical architecture
that inspired him to design and build Wilbury.

He also became interested in garden design, particularly hydraulics, and carried
out a project to bring piped water to Shaftesbury in Dorset. The works were actually
designed by the curate of Shaftesbury, Mr Holland. But Benson took the credit. As a
result, the grateful residents elected him as their MP in 1715, but at a later election he
failed to be returned – and promptly cut off the water supply.

Benson ingratiated himself with George I, travelling with him to his palace of
Herrenhausen in Hanover, where he was commissioned to build a fountain in the
famous gardens there. The fountain failed to produce the promised impressive *jet d'eau*
and managed only a damp squib. In 1718, Benson took over from Christopher Wren as
Surveyor of the King's Works, helped into the post by various political allies. During his
tenure, he alienated most of his colleagues. He finally overreached himself by insisting
that the House of Lords was in danger of imminent collapse and needed immediate
repairs. This false claim resulted, not surprisingly, in his dismissal.

However, despite his many misdemeanours, he remained a good friend of the Hoare
family. Good Henry stayed with Benson while he was looking for a property to buy.
Encouraged by Benson, he decided on the estate and house at Stourton.

Investing in bricks and mortar, and especially in land, not only provided a safe place for the Hoares' money, but also raised their status. Customers of the bank could feel confident that the family had land and property behind them, and Henry could begin to associate with the landed gentry – itself another source of clients and future profits. Victoria Hutchings has written:

> His purchase of the Stourton estate propelled the Hoare family from their membership of the merchant classes into the ranks of the landed gentry and his building of a neo-Palladian villa put them in the vanguard of good taste.[1]

This estate had been the property of the Stourton family since 1428, when John Stourton was given a licence to impark 1,000 acres. By the time Henry was interested in the estate, it had suffered ravages at the hands of the Parliamentarians during the Civil War: the Stourtons were Royalist and Catholic, and Stourton was a Royalist stronghold. Under the command of General Ludlow, the Parliamentarians had ransacked the existing house and made it uninhabitable. Ludlow was born in Maiden Bradley, the next village to Stourton; this was so typical of the Civil War, neighbour fighting neighbour, friend against friend.

Henry, then, made a shrewd purchase. He saw the potential offered by both house and estate. The first thing he did was to pull down the old-fashioned, dilapidated house and commission a smart, new replacement in the Palladian style, which was just becoming the latest fashion. In fact, Stourhead is one of the first houses to be built in this style: Wanstead House in Essex and Mereworth Castle in Kent were contemporary with Stourhead. All three houses were designed by the Scottish architect, Colen Campbell.

Henry may have been introduced to Campbell by William Benson. He may also have heard of this fashionable architect from Lord Burlington, who was Campbell's patron; both Burlington and Campbell had accounts at the bank. With an eye to potential wealthy clients, Campbell rather grandly named his portfolio of work *Vitruvius Britannicus*, referencing the first-century Roman architect, Vitruvius. It was a clever bit of marketing: Campbell knew that his potential clients understood everything that the name implied. Subscribers to the publication included the Duke and Duchess of Montagu, the Duke of Devonshire, the Earl of Pembroke; architects Henry Flitcroft and Thomas Archer; and Charles Bridgeman, the gardener. But ordinary working people also subscribed: Mr Thomas Churchill, bricklayer, for example, along with engravers and booksellers – and a few women, subscribing in their own right.

We can see how proud Henry is of his country villa in the portrait he commissioned which depicts him holding a plan that shows the elevation of the house. This portrait hangs in the Entrance Hall.

Two years after buying the Stourton estate, Henry decided to purchase the lease of a property in Quarley, a village halfway between Stourhead and London and not far from William Benson's house at Newton Tony. Hoare's bank archive holds a lease dated 13th October 1719, from the Hospital of St Katherine by the Tower in London, for the manor of Quarley, Southampton, for twenty-one years at a rent of £30 per annum.[2] The property at Quarley gave Henry a convenient place to stay while the house at Stourhead was being built.

Three months earlier, acting for William Benson, Henry had bought land at Grateley, the next village to Quarley. The Partnership private ledger at the Bank shows an entry:[3]

23rd June 1719   To Mr. Mountaine for the Purchase   £800
of lands at Greatsley [sic]

I'd heard about the existence of the house at Quarley but knew nothing about it. When it came to research, this, too, was seemingly a neglected area.

I decided to see what I could find out.

The first thing to do was to 'walk the walk' and visit the village of Quarley. I asked Anne if she would like to come with me. I got in touch with the parish council and found the Chair of the Council, Joanna Ferguson to be helpful and most interested in my reasons for visiting Quarley. She was happy to meet us and show us round, and willing to tell us all she could about the Hoare family's connection to the village. She also put us in touch with Desmond Graves, a local historian. Desmond kindly invited us for lunch and was a mine of information. We then enjoyed tea and conversation with Joanna. They could not have been more welcoming and forthcoming with their knowledge, and we learnt a lot from that visit.

The lovely little church, in immaculately kept grounds, contained a Venetian window that had been installed and paid for by Henry and Benson, their names carved into the sill:

Gulielmus Benson & Henricus Hoare Arm. A.D. 1723

At this date, Stourhead house was well on the way to being finished, but there was still much to be done furnishing the interior. Good Henry left £3,000 in his will for this purpose. On completion of Stourhead, his son, Henry the Magnificent, stayed at Quarley himself, with his wife, Susan, and their young children, when visiting the country; most of the time, of course, he lived in London. He was a member of the Quarley Hunt, enjoying the company of his young friends and his favourite sport, fox hunting.

Standing in the church porch, we looked across to where the house would have been. Today it is just a small field with uneven ground and several lumps and bumps. Next to this rough ground is the village hall, built in a slight depression. Desmond gave me a copy of the 1803 tithe map of Quarley. A fairly large pond is marked in this position, near to the house and close to the road. Apparently, the village hall still suffers from damp problems to this day.

We then walked down the road to Bridge Cottage, but there wasn't a bridge anywhere to be seen. Desmond had given us a copy of an article printed in a Hampshire magazine dated November 1987. This made the point that there wasn't a river or a railway in the vicinity which might have needed a bridge, so why the name 'Bridge Cottage'?

The article was written by a local man, Eric Levell, and was headed with the somewhat unlikely title, 'The Ex-cu-vitter'. Eric described an event which had taken place when he was a schoolboy:

> Stand with your back to Bridge Cottage with the humpity-bumpity meadow on your right and look half to the left where you will see a little field which was once the kitchen garden of the mansion and a humped back bridge carried the old flint road over a brick-built passageway under the road which led from the house to the garden.

There followed a hilarious account of the day an 'ex-cu-vitter' came to demolish the old bridge. Eric and his pals watched with trepidation as this fearsome monster in all 'its mucky magnificence' belched smoke, rumbling and clanking and waving about the big iron bucket, complete with the *pièce de résistance*, 'a pair of caterpillar tracks'. The children had never seen anything like it. They asked the workmen, "What is it?" "What is it?" repeated the man. "Why 'tis an ex-cu-vitter and they'm goin' to dig up the ole bridge." Much to their amazement and delight, they were even permitted to watch the goings-on in the afternoon, instead of sitting in the classroom. Their teacher accompanied them; she must have secretly wanted to watch this herself and later used it as a topic. Eric Levell ends by saying:

> In due course a new piece of road was made across the scar left by the removal of the bridge ... then nature was left to repair the banks and grow the grass so that by all but a very few of us the bridge was forgotten.

Standing outside Bridge Cottage, looking down the road, we tried to imagine the mansion on the right and the bridge with a brick-built tunnel underneath, leading to a small garden on the left. This tunnel gave the family and their gardeners easy access from the house to their garden, without inconveniencing neighbours by closing the road.

Then a flash of inspiration struck us. Could this arrangement have been in Henry's mind when he created Rock Arch at Stourhead? All those years earlier, as a young man, he would have used the tunnel under the road to access the other part of his Quarley garden. Many years later, he was looking for a way of solving the problem of how to lead visitors out of the garden and up to the Temple of Apollo, without closing the road to local people. Perhaps he remembered how well this arrangement at Quarley worked. He used the decorative feature of Rock Arch to take visitors up the hill to the Temple of Apollo, and then brought them back into the garden via a tunnel which he named the Souterrain. Visitors would not realise they were briefly leaving the garden. The design trick had the added advantage of keeping the road open for villagers and the general public.

Admittedly, this is conjecture, but the idea seems entirely plausible. It's only by visiting sites and 'walking the walk' that these little flashes of recognition present themselves.

Both Joanna and Desmond suggested we should visit Hampshire Record Office, in Winchester, where we might find additional information. So, fired with enthusiasm, we decided to go and have a look. We were particularly on the lookout for any references to Francis Faugoin working in the gardens at Quarley or Grateley.

Our visit revealed two documents describing Quarley Manor. One was dated 1756, but the other did not have a date and was in poor condition; it was torn and difficult to read. However, the description of the manor in the two documents was almost identical. This is what the 1756 document stated:

> The Mansion House called Quarley House in the Parish of Quarley aforesaid, being a very ancient and decayed building of about Six Rooms on a floor with a Dovehouse, Stables and other Outhouses, a large Yard and a little Walled Garden of about a quarter of an acre and Orchard and a small piece of Pasture Ground adjoining containing in the whole about four Acres.[4]

The same words described the manor in the older document, except that it stated 'an ancient building of about Six Rooms', omitting the word 'decayed'. So, we assumed that this document was older, as at this time the house was not 'decayed'.

We also found a detailed map showing the manor of Grateley and Grateley Lodge. This map was dated 1790, and stated that it was the property of William Benson Earle, the grandson of William Benson, brother-in-law of Good Henry.

We knew that Henry had purchased land at Grateley on behalf of Benson. As only 'land' was mentioned, we didn't know if the manor house shown on this map was existing at the time and later extended and improved, or whether Benson built it from scratch. However, we did know from looking at the map that it was a substantial establishment.

The mansion house was set back from the road, an imposing gateway giving access to a courtyard. It had many outbuildings, a formal garden and what appeared to be an orchard. Just down the road, on a corner, a large field was marked with the words 'Hoares Barn'. We also found a later map of the Parish of Grateley dated 1837, but there was no trace of Grateley Lodge. It had completely disappeared from the map.

Our investigations had revealed much useful information about Quarley and Grateley. But, sadly, our visit to the record office had not resulted in finding any documents relating to Francis Faugoin. We still had to find out why he was described on his marriage record as 'Batchelor of Grateley'. If he was described thus on the record, he must have lived there. So, we could only assume he must have been employed by Benson at Grateley Lodge, possibly also working for Henry at Quarley House. Although it made sense to place Francis working for Benson at Grateley, we had no firm evidence to support the idea.

It was back to the drawing board.

1 Hutchings, Victoria. *Messrs. Hoare Bankers: A History of the Hoare Banking Dynasty.* Constable & Robinson Ltd, London, 2005. p. 47.

2 C. Hoare & Co. archive: HE/1/A/21.

3 Partnership ledger, Henry Hoare's private account (Feb. 1718). C. Hoare & Co. archive.

4 Hampshire Record Office, Winchester. 3M54/7.

CHAPTER FIVE

JOHN FAUGOIN, 'GARDINER' AT DITTON

H AVING DRAWN A blank at Hampshire Record Office, we decided to take a different approach. Presuming Francis Faugoin was French, and looking at his dates, there was a possibility his family were Huguenot refugees.

France, unlike England, was a Catholic country; the Huguenots were French Protestants. The right to practise their religion was protected by law when Henri IV issued the Edict of Nantes in 1598, giving them considerable privileges on condition they did not try to convert others. In 1685, however, Louis XIV – the Sun King – revoked the Edict of Nantes, outlawing the practice of Protestantism in France. Severe persecution followed. King Charles II offered sanctuary to the Huguenots, and between 40,000 and 50,000 people, from all walks of life, sought refuge in England. They travelled at great personal risk; it was forbidden by law to leave France.

France's loss was England's gain. Most Huguenots had the means to pay their passage; they had skills they could take with them and were confident in their abilities to find work. They were well educated, hard-working and talented. For obvious reasons, they preferred at first to stay together in their own communities. Not only was their language different, but also the way they dressed, and even the food they ate, made them stand out. The weaving community that settled in Spitalfields in London is well known.

Jean contacted the Huguenot Society. Although they were not able to throw any light on the name 'Faugoin', they sent a copy of an article written for the Society by Tessa Murdoch. I discovered that Tessa Murdoch was Deputy Keeper of Sculpture, Metalwork, Ceramics and Glass at the Victoria and Albert Museum (V&A) in London. Her article gave much information about the Dukes of Montagu and their patronage of Huguenot craftsmen. The first duke, Ralph Montagu, was appointed Ambassador to Louis XIV, and when visiting France, was entertained by Louis at Versailles. His son, the second duke, John Montagu, employed Huguenot stewards, silversmiths, artists and furniture makers at the family home, Boughton House in Northamptonshire. Murdoch's article listed several of these artisans, and one name jumped out at us: 'John Faugoin, Gardiner at Ditton'.

We couldn't quite believe it. Who was John Faugoin? And where was Ditton?

The only information we had up to this point was the inscription on the grave in the churchyard at Stourhead – giving the names of Francis and his wife Mary – and their marriage record. With John's name, Jean was able to start work on establishing a family tree.

Her research uncovered the fascinating story of Francis's family. It turned out that he came from a whole family of gardeners.

John was Francis's father; his wife Susannah, was Francis's mother. John and Susannah had seven children: Charles baptised in 1702; John baptised in 1704; Elizabeth baptised in 1708 in Twickenham, at the church of St Mary the Virgin; Susanna in 1710, Jane in 1712 and Francis followed in 1716. The last son, Henry, was baptised on 15th June 1718 at Stoke Poges. Henry married Elizabeth Larkin in 1753 at St Paul's Cathedral; they had three children. Henry was described in the marriage register as 'Gardener'.

I now contacted Tessa Murdoch, explaining the reasons for my interest in John Faugoin. She kindly gave me contact details for Nicola Hopkinson, Personal Assistant to the Duke of Buccleuch. While the Duke's main residence is Boughton House in Northamptonshire, at the time, Ditton House belonged to his ancestor, the Duke of Montagu. In addition, Nicola gave me an introduction to an archivist who had recently joined the team at Boughton, Crispin Powell.

Murdoch also let me have contact details for Susan Tomkins, archivist to Lord Montagu of Beaulieu. Susan Tomkins was extremely helpful and encouraging. To my delight she told me that there were three maps held at Beaulieu dated 1718, 1725 and 1742. Apparently, these were not the originals but good-quality reproductions. These three maps showed the garden at Ditton, and she sent me the digital images.

I then contacted Crispin Powell at Boughton. Little did I know at the time, but Crispin was an experienced archivist, who had previously worked for twenty-two years at Northamptonshire Record Office, and who, I like to think, was to become quite a friend over the years. It was one of those serendipitous happenings: Crispin had just been taken on as archivist, with responsibility for cataloguing the Montagu archive at Boughton. I was his first 'customer', so to speak, in his new role. He told me that a considerable portion of the Montagu archive was stored at Northamptonshire Record Office, and suggested I should pay a visit there.

To my astonishment, the name of John Faugoin was quite familiar to him: he had seen it many times in documents and ledgers relating to the house and garden at Ditton Park, which was one of the homes of the Montagus. Ditton Park was near the village of Datchet, beside the Thames and close to Windsor. Crispin went on to explain that John Faugoin's name appeared in the accounts kept by the steward at Ditton Park, Andrew Marchant. These accounts also referred to 'new work' being done under John's supervision in the early 1720s. Apparently, John Faugoin was still employed at Ditton in the late 1730s.

Crispin also suggested I should look at a map of Ditton Park and house, dated 1695, by the surveyor, William Aldersey.

Receiving all this unexpected flood of information was one of those key moments that make research so fascinating and enjoyable. A trip to Northamptonshire Record Office was essential, to see these documents and especially the 1695 map. Luckily, my sister, Vicky, lives in Northamptonshire, so I was able to stay with her. As a result, I had the opportunity of spending two days at the record office. My sister came along as she was equally intrigued, and I was grateful for her help: she had an eagle eye.

Unfortunately, Crispin was away at the time of our visit, but left instructions for where to find the 1695 map. He said I was the first person to ask to see it, which seemed to amuse him. I was hopeful that we would meet at some point in the future.

At the same time, I contacted Buckinghamshire Record Office to find out if they had anything of use. They put me in touch with a local historian, Janet Kennish. Fortunately for us, Janet was another huge source of information about Ditton and nearby Datchet, having studied the history of the area and the families over many years. She was most willing to share her knowledge and confirmed that Jane Faugoin was baptised in Datchet on 17th August 1712. As Jane's husband, Joseph Cantrell, is buried in the churchyard of St Mary the Virgin in Datchet, it may be safe to assume that she is buried in the same churchyard. Janet then gave us another remarkable fact: John Faugoin, too, is buried there. She could even show us his grave. She sent a photo of the headstone. We couldn't believe our luck.

The headstone had an ornate, scrolled top and featured the head of a cherub enfolded by angel's wings, long trumpets and, at each side, the flared leaves of some kind of plant. The inscription beneath read:

M. John Faugoin late of Ditton Park died Apr 23rd 1743 age 77.
A tender father, a good husband & a good neighbour, erected by his son Henry.

What a lovely inscription. Such heartfelt words by his son gave us a wonderful description of the man, as a loving father and husband and someone who valued his friends and neighbours. I also noted that he was recorded not as 'Mr John Faugoin', but as 'M. John Faugoin'.

Janet added that she had a complete copy of the transcribed parish registers. The only Faugoin baptism was of Jane, parents John and Susannah – their names not appearing in the marriage registers. The fact that a marriage record didn't exist in the Datchet parish registers indicated that their marriage took place elsewhere.

Jean soon found the record. It stated that they were married in London, at the church of St Mary Abbotts in Kensington, on 15th November 1700. John was thirty-four years old. It also gave us another name: Susannah's maiden name, le Cerf. John was described as 'Gardener of Hammersmith' and Susannah as 'Servant of this Parish'. Jean later found the will of Susannah's brother, Charles le Cerf,[1] in which he was described as 'Gardener of Putney'. Traditionally, the firstborn child would have been named after one or other parent, but as John and Susannah called their firstborn Charles,

Charles le Cerf must have been important to them – above and beyond being Susannah's brother. As expected, their second son was named John, after his father and their second daughter, Susannah, after her mother.

Jean also obtained a copy of John's will from The National Archives at Kew.[2] He left one hundred pounds to each of his children, and the residue of his estate, personal goods and household furniture to his wife. It also gave another useful snippet of information. John had written his will in French, as it was stated: 'Faithfully translated out of French ... by me, P. Crespigny'.

John's will gave the name of two witnesses: Lazarus Merry and Edmond Carter. Janet Kennish told us that Lazarus Merry was a member of a long-established Ditton yeoman family, and that Edmond Carter was one of the most prominent farmers in Datchet, and a member of the Carter family of sculptors. This was interesting: a later member of the Carter family, Benjamin Carter, carved the reliefs in the Pantheon at Stourhead.

This further added to the picture we were beginning to build of John and his family. One of John's closest friends was a successful farmer and a member of a talented and famous family of sculptors, so Francis would have grown up knowing of the Carters. Janet said the Carter family remained based in Datchet while working in London and elsewhere, and all the family were brought back to Datchet for burial. There are memorials to the family in the church.

Susannah's will[3] also provided an interesting little insight. She named Francis and his sister Jane as executors of her will, dividing her estate between all her children and grandchildren and stating: 'I give to the Poor Housekeepers of Ditton aforesaid each a peck loaf or Two Shillings and Six pence in Lieu thereof as they shall choose'. The family was clearly prosperous enough to enable Susannah to leave money to the poor of the parish, people she would have known well. She also directed that 'I desire to be decently and privately buryed [sic] near my late Husband in Datchett [sic] Church'. Janet thought there was a strong possibility that Susannah was buried in the same grave as John (as she had directed in her will). She suspected her inscription was on the same headstone, but lower down, so that it was now obscured by turf. She explained that when the face of the headstone next to John's grave was cleared of turf, a hitherto completely hidden inscription was revealed, and that this could well be the case with John's headstone.

Janet continued by saying that the family were much more likely to have lived at Ditton than in Datchet village and were only buried at the churchyard in Datchet because there was no churchyard at Ditton hamlet's chapel. Much later, we learned that the tiny private chapel in the grounds of Ditton House had a French Huguenot priest.

A rich picture was now emerging. Francis grew up in a large French Huguenot family, with loving and respected parents, three brothers and three sisters. It was a family of gardeners: Francis's uncle and younger brother were both gardeners, and his father, John, worked as head gardener for the Duke of Montagu at Ditton House. Francis took the same career path, but he was the only one to move away from the London area, to live and work in Stourton, Wiltshire.

We began to reflect that Francis Faugoin came from a gardening family and Henry Hoare from a banking family. Their family values shaped the men they were to become.

We felt that progress was being made. The next step was to discover what John Faugoin was employed to do at Ditton House.

1 Charles le Cerf will, 1735. The National Archives of the UK, Kew, Richmond, London TW9 4DU (TNA): PROB 11/671/451.

2 John Faugoin will, 1743. TNA: PROB 11/728/167.
3 Susannah Faugoin will, 1757. TNA: PROB 11/828/130.

CHAPTER SIX

DITTON PARK

D ITTON PARK WAS close to Windsor, with access by ferry to Westminster from Datchet across the Thames . The Ditton house and garden are enclosed by a moat. This is where John Faugoin was employed as a gardener.

Ditton Park belonged to Sir Ralph Winwood (1563–1617), Secretary of State to James I. Many of Sir Ralph's contemporaries were keen gardeners, amongst them Henry Fanshawe (1569–1616) of Ware Park and Sir Christopher Hatton (1540–1591) from Kirby Hall in Northamptonshire. Lady Fanshawe is quoted as saying that the travel writer William Camden (1551–1623) described Ware Park as 'unsurpassed in England for its flowers, physic-herbs and fruits'. According to the letters of John Chamberlain (1554–1628), Fanshawe received plants from Sir Ralph's garden at Ditton.[1]

The Ditton Park estate passed to the Montagu family through Sir Ralph's daughter, Anne (d. 1643), who married Edward Montagu. Their son, Ralph (1638–1709), was the first Duke of Montagu. In 1666, he was honoured with the appointment of Ambassador to Louis XIV, a most prestigious position. A contemporary Huguenot writer and historian who settled in London, Abel Boyer, described a visit by Montagu:

> His publick Entry in Paris was so Magnificent that it has scarce ever been since equalled. He rode in the State Coach of the King of France and was accompanied by more than a hundred attendants riding in Four Rich Coaches with Eight Horses each and Two Chariots with six, made as fine and as costly as Art and Workmen could contrive.[2]

Whenever Ralph Montagu visited Versailles, Louis XIV ordered the fountains to be played. These visits strongly influenced the Duke: when he redesigned his Northamptonshire house, Boughton, he added a new north front to the original Tudor manor in the style of Versailles. Indeed, Boughton became known as 'the English Versailles'. He also set about creating a grand formal garden around the house, featuring parterres, canals, water basins and fountains. Apparently, he had problems with the management of the water: 'ye water with which he had hoped to make so fine fountains, hath failed his expectations'.[3] Louis XIV had the same problems at Versailles. The design for the Boughton garden can be seen in Colen Campbell's portfolio of designs, *Vitruvius Britannicus*. Volume III of the portfolio also contains the design for the house at Stourhead.

The Duke was impressed by the talented artists, craftsmen and designers employed by the Sun King, many of them Huguenots. He personally encouraged some of them to come to London and work under his patronage. He commissioned beautiful still-life flower paintings by the Huguenot Jean-Baptiste Monnoyer, their giltwood frames being designed by the Pelletier family. Peter Rieusset, joiner, supplied a billiard table and frame with turned feet for Ditton Park in October 1702. Daniel Marot, furniture designer and engraver, came to England with William III. His name is found in the account books of Ralph Montagu, and Marot is described in the Boughton guidebook as 'the guiding spirit behind both Boughton and Montagu House'.

In her article, 'The Dukes of Montagu as Patrons of the Huguenots', Tessa Murdoch comments:

> Three successive generations of the Montagu family recognized the potential of the Huguenot refugees and their descendants and Boughton House, its contents and its archives provide a remarkable witness to their enlightened patronage.[4]

Duke Ralph's son, John (1690–1749), inherited the estates and, like his father, continued to patronise Huguenot craftsmen. He was educated by Huguenot tutors and spoke fluent French. Significantly, his household was run by Huguenot stewards, Elias de Rit and Marc Antonie. He also opened an account with Hoare's Bank, which was only closed by his executors at his death – a period of nearly fifty years. There is another connection with the Hoare family: the Duke sold his New Hall estate to Henry's uncle Benjamin, in 1730.

Did Duke John recommend the son of his head gardener at Ditton to Henry Hoare?

Duke John's great passion was planting trees and improving gardens, both at Boughton and at Ditton House. He designed the great water features at Boughton and undertook extensive 'new works' at Ditton. He planted avenues of limes at Boughton; at Ditton, he planted hundreds of trees and a circle of elms, which enhanced the approach to the drawbridge over the moat. His nickname was 'Planter' John.

From the documents we had consulted on our visit to Northamptonshire Record Office, my sister, Vicky, and I were slowly able to build a good picture of John Faugoin as the 'Gardiner' employed at Ditton: his responsibilities; the work done and paid for; the accounts he kept; the trees planted; and the wages paid to the labourers, and those he received himself.

The first thing to see was the wonderful map of Ditton Park, dated 1695. This showed a small drawing of the house in the centre, surrounded by the garden and moat, all set within the wider park. The mansion looked to have tall Tudor chimneys, together with later, Dutch-style, William and Mary gables. This was more than I could have hoped for: a drawing of the façade of Ditton House, albeit not the one we see today. It was helpful to understand what the garden looked like then, so that we could appreciate how much Duke John altered it over the years. The scale and variety of the changes highlighted the amount of work undertaken. It also demonstrated John Faugoin's ability to oversee these changes. And, of course, his son Francis would have grown up witnessing all this activity.

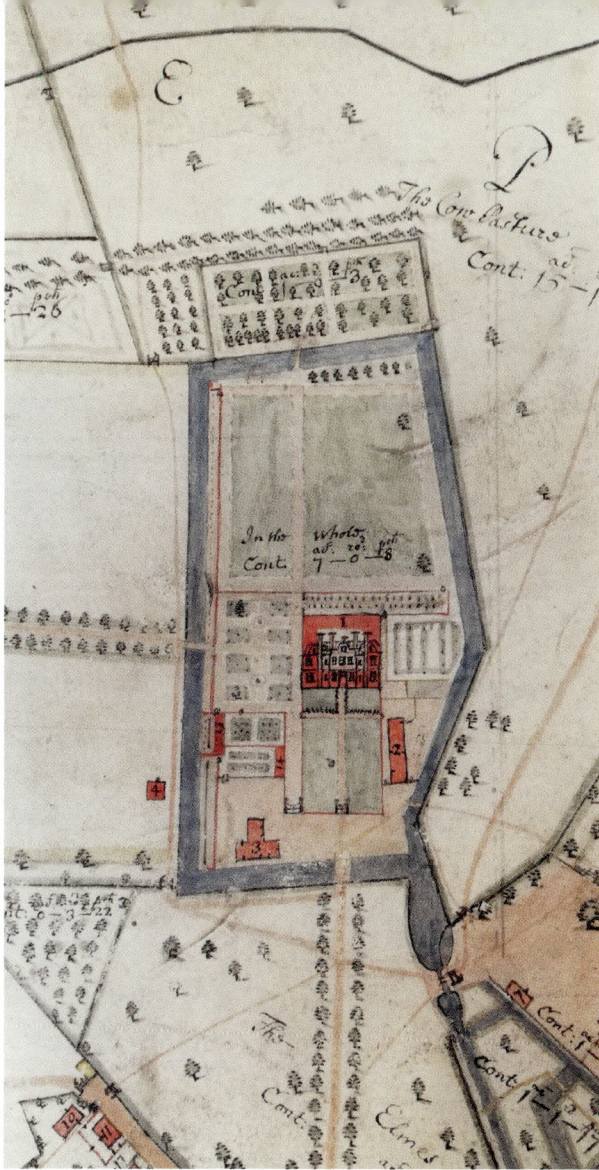

Detail 1695 map showing Ditton house surrounded by a moat
Buccleuch Archives | By kind permission of the Duke of Buccleuch and Queensberry, KT

THE GARDEN IN 1695

The 1695 map shows Ditton House, set within Ditton Park, surrounded by a moat. The approach to the front entrance was from the east, along a straight double avenue of trees leading to a bridge over the moat. The area surrounding the house is shown in detail. Within the confines of the moat, brick walls enclosed geometric spaces: lawns, trees and flower beds. A straight path led to the front door; this path was flanked by four lawns. The two smaller lawns nearest the house were bounded by iron railings, the whole enclosed by brick walls with decorative gateways.

On the right when facing the house, outbuildings contained the dairy, laundry, workhouse and brewhouse. On the left, a walled enclosure contained what the map calls the 'Old Orange House' and the 'New Orange House'. Surprisingly close to the house are the slaughterhouse, stables and coach house and, beyond the moat, in the words of the map, the 'Pidgeon [sic] House'. There were more formal square beds, possibly containing fruit trees in a quincunx pattern.

The development of the garden can be traced with the help of three further maps dated 1718, 1725 and 1742. Digital images of these maps were kindly sent to me by Susan Tomkins, archivist to Lord Montagu of Beaulieu.

THE GARDEN IN 1718

In 1718 John Faugoin was fifty-two years old and Francis was two.

John began to work for Duke John in 1718: his name appeared in that year, in both the Antonie accounts and the Marchant accounts. The first record of his employment was in the Antonie accounts: '1st February 1718 – Mr. Faugoin on Account, £25 0s 0d'. Mark Antonie was the Duke's chief steward, and Andrew Marchant was the London house steward. They succeeded one another at Ditton, as the Ditton estate was then small enough to have been managed from the London town house.

The garden and house were remodelled from 1700 to 1705. By 1718, the garden had changed dramatically. All the outbuildings had been swept away. An oval lawn at the front entrance had made an appearance, together with many more formal areas of planting and parterres. The biggest change, however, was the huge area of trees planted beyond the moat to the south, with many criss-crossing paths. In the 18th century, large areas of formally planted trees were referred to as a 'wilderness'. The main axis through the wilderness was aligned on the south side of the house. Inside the moat, to the north-west, were three straight paths radiating from a round feature, possibly a temple. This type of configuration was called a 'goosefoot'. Finally, the avenue of trees leading to the bridge across the moat had been replaced by a double circle of elms. The Antonie accounts show a delivery of 100 elms to Ditton on 28th November 1717 for £15.

THE GARDEN IN 1725

By 1725, John Faugoin was fifty-nine years old, and Francis was nine.

There had been large-scale changes over the intervening seven years. All the formal areas had been swept away. All that remained of the wilderness was the axial avenue of trees and those which delineated the boundaries. The goosefoot was still there (but the round structure had disappeared), and the circle of elms also remained in place. What has suddenly made a dramatic appearance is the presence of an oddly shaped lake to the north-west. This seems to have been developed from an existing rectangular basin, which was present even in 1695 and could possibly have been part of a medieval fishpond complex.

The lake at Ditton appeared quite large and contained an island with a fort. Duke John was a soldier on active service and became Master-General of the Ordnance. He fought alongside his son-in-law, John Churchill. Maybe he enjoyed mock battles on the lake, a popular pastime amongst military-minded aristocrats. It's an intriguing structure and it would be wonderful to find some contemporary sketches. There is, however, a reference to the fort in a letter written by John Chardin.

Sir John Chardin lived at Kempton Manor House on his estate at Sunbury-on-Thames. He was the son of a famous father, also Sir John Chardin (1643–1713), a wealthy French jeweller. This Sir John had travelled to the Near East and Persia in 1673 and, after a decade of travelling, returned to Europe. However, he left France as a persecuted Huguenot. He became jeweller to King Charles II and was later knighted. He wrote a ten-volume book entitled *The Travels of Sir John Chardin*.

In a letter dated 13th January 1733, the younger Sir John Chardin wrote to Duke John, extending a cordial invitation to visit his home whenever he desired. In this letter, he expressed the wish to visit Ditton in the summer and, remembering a previous visit, said:

> Next summer it will be delightful to pay my respects at Ditton as I did the last for that enchanted Island, fortifications, Tents, Cabins, drawbridge, ferryboat and ferryman is never to be forgot ...[5]

So, there is written evidence of the island and the fort that are clearly shown on the map. John Chardin also mentions 'Tents'. Could these be Turkish tents, which were popular at the time?

It's intriguing to think that, as a young boy, Francis would have known that his father had received instructions from the Duke to begin working on the creation of this new lake. He would have seen his father organising labour and materials and, no doubt, watched with interest as the new lake took shape, complete with an island. Little did Francis know at the time, but this experience would stand him in good stead later in his life.

All in all, the 1725 map is showing work in progress. John Faugoin had overseen the establishment of all these extensive new works since starting to work for the Duke in 1718.

THE GARDEN IN 1742

In 1742 John Faugoin was seventy-six. Francis was twenty-six and had already begun working for Henry Hoare.

We now have the finished garden as it was in Duke John's time. It had taken twenty-four years, from 1718 to 1742, for him to achieve his ambitious plans for the garden. It must have looked impressive.

Features that have remained since 1725 are the goosefoot, the circular planting of elms and the double-planted avenue of trees beyond the moat. The oval lawn in front of the house has made a re-appearance, and the lake with the island remains. The most significant change, however, has been the addition of many more large and stunning water features. The largest is a semi-circular expanse of water beyond the moat on north side. There is a new bridge across the moat, allowing people to walk across and round the new lake.

There are three small basins linked together to the west of the house. I was interested to see this configuration of three linked basins set in a rectangular area of planting: this design was also used at Boughton, shown on the 1722 *Vitruvius Britannicus* plan. Duke John must have liked the effect and introduced it to Ditton sometime between 1725 and 1742, when this map was made.

Francis was brought up seeing a garden laid out in the 'old' style – goosefoot, wilderness, parterre – and went on to help layout a garden in the 'new' style: naturalistic and fluid, not constrained by the straitjacket of symmetry and formality. Surely this was an unusual aspect of his story. At a pivotal moment in the development of the English landscape style – the transition from formal to informal – father and son helped to create *both* styles. As far as I know, this relationship has not been documented before in other gardens of this period.

John Faugoin was married in 1700 in London, when he was thirty-four. So, what was he doing between 1700 and 1718 when he began working for Duke John? We know that he lived at Hammersmith (as shown in the marriage record), but further clues can be found in a letter dated 15th April 1741 from the Ditton steward, Samuel Montagu. Crispin Powell sent me a digital image of this letter. Sam Montagu is responding to a request by the Duke, enquiring where he might purchase a laburnum. Sam Montagu relays the advice given by Faugoin:

> I've talked with the gardener about the flowering shrub called a laburnum and he saith there is none at Ditton nor in no gardens here abouts that ever he was in, he raised some when he was at Hammersmith and then some at Twitenham some years ago when he lived there, and is of opinion the likeliest place to get them is at the nurseries near London.

This letter confirms that John Faugoin was working at Hammersmith, which was the centre of the capital's nursery trade: he states that he 'raised' some, in other words propagated them. Laburnum was regarded as a rare shrub and was much sought after by keen plant collectors. Crispin added that Faugoin must have been quite a capable man: the gardens at Ditton were very much at the cutting edge in Duke John's time and contained many 'exotic' plants. 'Exotic' was the term used for non-native plants that were coming into London from all corners of the globe. Their cultural requirements were unknown, especially whether they would survive in the British climate.

According to Crispin, the gardens at Ditton Park were also possibly important horticultural showpieces, because the house itself was the setting for the Duke's 'house parties'. The eclectic range of guests included members of the aristocracy such as the Earls of Pembroke and Cardigan, and Lord Edgcumbe, as well as gentlemen of distinction and leading thinkers of the time: William Stukeley, the physician and antiquarian, who pioneered methods of accurately recording Stonehenge and Avebury; and Henry Baker, the naturalist, who published *The Microscope made Easy* in 1743. The guest list even included the great Sir Isaac Newton himself. Today we would call these men 'botanists', 'archaeologists' and 'scientists', but in the 18th century there was no such division. These men were all fascinated by what they called 'natural philosophy': they conducted experiments, recorded what they saw and shared their knowledge.

Invitations to the parties at Ditton Park were much sought after. There were no house rules; guests could come and go as they wished. This informality allowed them to mingle freely and engage in discussions and experiments, regardless of rank. Henry Baker commented:

> ... our evenings are usually spent together in making experiments till ten o'clock when we are called to supper.

Crispin added that these experiments often used plants as part of their discussions. He recalled that on one occasion they electrified a potted myrtle tree!

Another of the guests was Philip Miller, from Chelsea. Miller (1691–1771) was the chief gardener at the Chelsea Physic Garden and a knowledgeable horticulturist. He corresponded with other botanists, and obtained plants from all over the world, many of which he cultivated for the first time. Peter Collinson, a fellow botanist and enthusiastic garden maker, commented: 'Miller has raised the reputation of the Chelsea Garden so much that it excels all the gardens of Europe for its amazing variety of plants.' In 1731, Miller published his work, *The Gardener's Dictionary containing the Methods of Cultivating and Improving the Kitchen Fruit and Flower Garden*. This proved a great success and ran to eight editions. For his work at Chelsea, he was elected as a Fellow of the Royal Society.

I was impressed and delighted to think that John Faugoin may have discussed with the great Philip Miller the acquisition, planting and care of new species. He must have carried out his demanding job with a great degree of skill and competence and, perhaps, curiosity and pride that these leading thinkers of the day involved him in their experiments. He would almost certainly have had interesting discussions with Francis and passed on these new ideas.

We'd learnt from all our investigations that John Faugoin was an experienced gardener and knowledgeable plantsman, and that he was responsible for managing the many changes to the Ditton garden over a long period of time. Francis grew up in this garden and at a young age experienced the life of a gardener working for a wealthy and visionary employer. He also had been well schooled in horticulture by his knowledgeable father and perhaps mixed with talented craftsmen.

It was at Ditton that Francis began to understand the importance of working hard, maintaining an employer's trust and commanding the respect of his workmen. All these attributes were to stand him in good stead for the future.

1 Thacker, Christopher. *The Genius of Gardening*. Wiedenfeld and Nicolson, 1994. p. 102.

2 Murdoch, Tessa. 'The Dukes of Montagu as Patrons of the Huguenots', *Proceedings of the Huguenot Society*, Vol. XXV, No. 4, 1992. p. 340.

3 *Guidebook Boughton House*. Heritage House Group Ltd, Derby, 2006. p. 76.

4 Murdoch Tessa. 'The Dukes of Montagu as Patrons of the Huguenots'. p. 353.

5 Ibid. p. 351.

Ditton House and Bridge | Photographs: the author

CHAPTER SEVEN

DITTON HOUSE GARDEN TODAY

HAVING BUILT UP a picture of Francis's early life, Anne, Jean and I were now keen to visit Ditton House and see what the garden looked like today. Would there be any traces of the garden created by Duke John?

There was one big problem. The grounds weren't open to the public.

Janet Kennish came to our rescue. She had on previous occasions contacted the owners of Ditton Park at the time, Computer Associates, an American multinational corporation with headquarters in New York. CA Technologies was acquired later by Broadcom, who subsequently put the whole site up for sale. Today, Ditton Park is a conference centre.

Fortunately, our visit was well before all this. Janet put me in touch with the Facilities Co-ordinator, who organised a meeting with the Head Gardener, Sarah Weston, and she agreed to show us round. This was a piece of good luck: we were given the privilege of a private tour of the garden. I think the gardeners were as keen to meet us as we were to meet them, because I was able to show them copies of the maps providing extra historical background. Sarah Weston was particularly interested to know about the existence of her predecessor, John Faugoin, and the subsequent links with Stourhead.

Our visit took place on a glorious day in the middle of June. We walked down the broad path leading from the front entrance of the huge glass modern office building and crossed a bridge into the garden surrounding the house. It was quite a strange feeling: having pored over the maps for so long, I felt that I would easily be able to visualise the old garden, but it was quite difficult to orientate myself. So much had changed.

The place to begin to try to work things out was the bridge over the moat outside the garden itself. With my back to the house, I walked under the imposing turreted and crenellated gateway, crossed the iron-railed bridge over the moat and then turned and looked back at the house. The moat, bridge and gateway are still in the same position as they were in 1695. I tried to imagine the circle of elms that had been standing where I was now standing; apparently, the trees had been lost to Dutch elm disease. The oval lawn in front of the house, as shown on the 1742 map, is still there, but now includes a small reflective pool surrounded by stone seats and attractive planting. Thereafter, the layout was more difficult to imagine; but Sarah was most helpful and, with the aid of the maps, we were able to discuss where some of the features might have been.

Although the garden had changed, the house was still there, but not the house John Faugoin knew. In 1812, fire destroyed the old house, and it was rebuilt to a design by the architect William Atkinson in the early Gothic Revival style, which was gaining popularity at that time. It is built of brick, covered by stucco painted a soft cream, with the trademark turrets and crenellations, reminiscent of Horace Walpole's Strawberry Hill at Twickenham.

J.C. Loudon, the eminent garden writer, visited in 1833 and reported in *The Gardener's Magazine*:

> The House which is castellated and was rebuilt a few years ago by Mr. Atkinson, is surrounded by a moat. It has altogether an excellent effect and there are a very appropriate chapel, gardener's house and two lodges.

What a pity the 'gardener's house' is no longer there. However, our guide took us to see a small, brick-built summerhouse by the side of the moat, which she felt sure would have been there in John's day. I was keen to see the chapel and the island. Sadly, the chapel, which was still intact, had been cordoned off, so we weren't able to go in. I was disappointed: this must have been where the Faugoin family worshipped.

Crispin Powell has receipts signed by the Rev. Henry Justel for officiating at the private chapel in the grounds. The Rev. Henry Justel was a Huguenot whose father, also called Henry, or Henri, had fled to England in 1681, well before the Revocation of Nantes in 1685. He was a great scholar and had held the position of Secretary to Louis XIV. He correctly read the intentions of Louis XIV and made up his mind to come to England, where he had many friends, the philosopher John Locke and writer John Evelyn among them. Having arrived in London, he soon became the Keeper of the King's Library at St James's Palace for Charles II. He died in September 1693 and is buried at Eton College. His son, the Rev. Henry, became chaplain to the Duke of Montagu and spent some of his time at Ditton.

A receipt for six months' officiating at Ditton's chapel is dated 26th November 1716, which is the year Francis was born. We were only able to calculate the year of his birth from the inscription on the grave, as Jean had not managed to find any baptism record. This was most frustrating: a baptism record would not only have confirmed the date but also may have noted details of his parents and possibly where they were living at the time.

Unfortunately, the island with the fort (shown on the 1725 and 1742 maps) was also fenced off, but easily visible and now overgrown with trees. It required a good deal of imagination to conjure up a picture of Heron Island, complete with fort, and the mock battles being fought on and off the water. Access to the island was via Gibraltar Bridge, presumably so named to commemorate the capture of Gibraltar in 1704 by the combined forces of the British and the Dutch during the War of the Spanish Succession.

It was with reluctance that we tore ourselves away from this special garden, surrounded by its moat of clear, gently flowing water. We felt that John's legacy was in good hands: the present garden team were keeping it in immaculate condition, and it retained a quiet, peaceful feeling.

We soon cheered up after a good lunch at the pub in Datchet and then went to see the next highlight: a grave. I seem to be rather fond of graves! This really was a highlight, to stand in front of John Faugoin's grave in Datchet and read the inscription: 'a tender father ...'. What a revealing choice of words, implying a kind-hearted and affectionate man, who set a fine example for Francis to follow. Looking at John's grave reminded me of standing in front of his son's grave at Stourhead. Thinking of the two of them was quite a poignant moment.

The whole trip had been so worthwhile. We felt it anchored John to a place, rather than his being just a name in the records. However, I was inspired to go back to the records and see if we could find out even more about John.

On our second visit to the Northamptonshire Record Office, Vicky and I had the pleasure of meeting Crispin for the first time. He'd already been helpful and encouraging; without his knowledge we would never have found out so much about John.

As I hoped, this second visit proved to be most useful, yielding lovely little insights into the life of a gardener of the early 18th century.

Crispin advised us to investigate the meticulous accounts kept by the Steward, Andrew Marchant. These gave details of work done in the garden at Ditton: wages for labourers; and board wages, an allowance for lodging and food provided to an employee as part of their wages. The earliest reference to John I could find was in February 1718, when Francis was two years old.

It was thrilling to be able to see so many references to John – and even his signature when he signed a receipt for wages.[1]

> Received the 12th October 1725 of his Grace the Duke of Montagu, by the Hands of Mr. Andrew Marchant, the sum of Nineteen Pounds two shillings paid in full for the half a year's Wages and Boardwages to Michaelmas Last; I say received | JOHN FAUGOIN

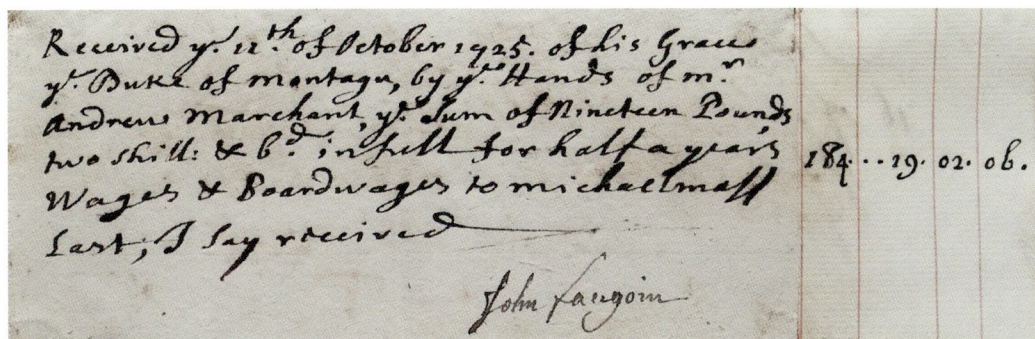

Receipt for wages signed by John Faugoin
Buccleuch Archives | By kind permission of the Duke of Buccleuch and Queensberry, KT

1726 Payment for the Gardens, Labourers and Wages[2]

3rd April	To Mr. Faugoin on account of wages	£4 7s 0d
17th July	Ditto for to pay Wages, Mowers, Haymakers	£17 17s 0d
18th Sept.	To Mr. Faugoin Quarter charges for Gardens	£25 4s 0d
29th Dec.	To Mr. Faugoin in full balance due Ladyday 1721	£2 9s 0d
	Ditto for to pay Labourers and Wages	£19 10s 0d

In that same year, 1726, on 19th January, there is an entry for Mrs Faugoin for 'joystment of a cow for 31 weeks – £2 6s 6d', 'joystment' being the renting of a cow. I even found an inventory of equipment used in the garden at Ditton in 1709, most of which we can still recognise today.[3]

34 Orange Trees	3 Prs. Sheers	Iron Rowler
110 Baye Trees	5 Rakes	2 Turfing Irons
20 Holly	a drag Nett	2 Edging Irons
4 stone Rowlers	a casting Nett	2 leaden figures and standes
3 wooden Rowlers	9 Bell Glasses	4 wooden seats
5 Hoes	5 Melon frames	
a Reel	A boat and skulls	

Total value: £189.00.00

Another discovery was a document dated 22nd June 1728, listing some of the people who worked for John.[4]

> We whose names underwriting [sic] do acknowledge to have received of his Grace the Duke of Montagu by the hand of John Faugoin the several sums wrote against our respective names is in full for working in Ditton Garden from 25th March 1728 to 16th June 1728.

There followed the names of Lazarus Merry and Edmond Carter, both of whom signed their names. Others acknowledged receipt of wages by marking with a cross. Merry and Carter were both personal friends of John.

However, the *pièce de résistance* was an entry in the name of Francis Faugoin at ten pence per day, totalling £1 17s 6d. It was a joy to see his youthful signature right there on the page in front of us: he was twelve years old. We suddenly realised that Francis was expected, even at this stage in his life, to do hands-on work in the garden to earn some money of his own. Another good example of the life lessons taught him by his father.

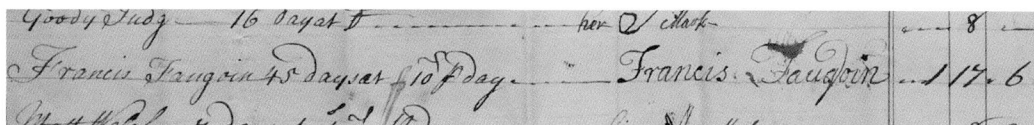

Document dated 22nd June 1728 showing Francis Faugoin, age 12, receiving wages for working in the garden
Buccleuch Archives | By kind permission of the Duke of Buccleuch and Queensberry, KT

The Establishment at Ditton.

	Wages.	B: Wages.	£	s.	d.
Mr. Sam Montagu, Steward there	✓40 ..	..			
Mr. Faugoin, Gardiner	✓20 ..	✓18	-5	--	
One Housmaid	✓.5 ..	✓15	12	--	
One Dairymaid	✓.5 ..	✓15	12	--	
One Groom	✓.8 ..	✓18	-4	--	
Porter	✓.8 ..	✓15	12	--	
1 Carter & Assistant to the Groom. Hen: Montagu	8 ..	✓18	-4	--	
1 Extra Cook & Assistant in the Kitchen when the Family is not there (about)	✓10 --	--- ..			
	✓104 ..	✓101 -9 ..			
	101 -9				
	205 -9 --		✓205	-9	--

Gardens.

			£	s.	d.
8 Men constantly employ'd to support the Gardens & new Works at 14 each ♯ day, 52 H.	✓145	12	--		
1 Weeder to keep the Courts & Walks clean	✓.7	16	6		
Garden Seeds, Nails, Nets, Tools & other Utensils	✓.10	4	--		
			✓163	12	6

			£	s.	d.
Kitchen, Expences on an average for the two last Years	---	--	✓172	-1	5
Stable, Expences ditto			✓213	-7	9
Carried over			£754	10	8

'The Establishment at Ditton' | By kind permission of the Duke of Buccleuch and Queensberry, KT

In another ledger accounting for wages at 'The Establishment at Ditton',[5] the list is headed by 'Mr. Sam Montagu, Steward there – £40', followed by 'Mr. Faugoin, Gardiner – £20, Boardwages £18 5s 0d', followed by 'One Housemaid ..., One Dairymaid ... One Groom ..., Porter'. This shows the status of John Faugoin: he is named immediately after the Steward and referred to as 'Mr'. He received half the wages of the Steward and, in addition, board wages. The other servants were not given a name, just their job title. It is striking that their wages were only £8 and £5 for the year, so much less than John's £20, but the board wages were similar.

In the receipt book for 11th March 1726, John Faugoin heads the page, receiving thirty-one guineas on account of Ditton House and Garden. This entry is followed by another receipt, dated 1st April, from a more famous name: Charles Bridgeman (1690–1738).[6] Often described as a garden designer who worked in the transitional period between the formal and the informal, Bridgeman was employed initially by Lord Cobham to lay out the first phase of the gardens at Stowe, and by Colonel Robert Dormer-Cottrell at Rousham. He also contributed to the early phase of the gardens surrounding Claremont House in Esher, Surrey, where he is credited with the design of an unusual stepped and turfed amphitheatre.

The ledger entry reads:

> Rec'd the 1st April of His Grace the Duke of Montagu by the hand of Mr. Andrew Marchant the Sum of Twenty-five pounds in full for keeping the Gardens at Montagu House to Ladyday last; I say received | CHARLES BRIDGEMAN

So, Bridgeman had responsibility for the Duke's garden at his London house. His signature was done with a great flourish. But he was paid only five pounds more than John Faugoin.

It is tempting to speculate that, although Bridgeman was employed at Montagu House, he may have visited Ditton House. I imagined John holding conversations with this fellow gardener, albeit a more famous one.

John Faugoin was still employed at Ditton in 1732, when he was sixty-six. He was paid a wage of £20 per annum plus board wages. The same record says that there were eight men working under him 'constantly employed to support the gardens and new works at 14d each per day'. He must have been fit and healthy to still be a useful employee at this age. He died on 23rd April 1743 at the ripe old age of seventy-seven, a respectable age even by today's standards.

On the day his father died, Francis was twenty-seven years old and married. He had started a family and was already employed by Henry Hoare at Quarley. John must have been proud of the fact that his son was working for a wealthy London banker. He had trained him well.

Francis grew up at Ditton Park. He witnessed his father keeping careful accounts, paying wages, planting trees and maintaining the garden in pristine condition. He was surrounded by talented French craftsmen who, like him, were Huguenots. He may have never ventured into the house, but he would surely have heard his father talking with the highly skilled craftsmen employed to furnish it. He was expected to work hard – from the age of twelve, or younger – and he could read and write.

He, was, therefore, well qualified to work for Henry the Magnificent. But how did Francis get from Ditton House to Stourhead?

1   Montagu archives, Boughton House: BM17.
2   Ibid.
3   Ibid.
4   Ibid.
5   Ibid.
6   Ibid.

CHAPTER EIGHT

FRANCIS FAUGOIN AND MARY SWETMAN

T HE ANSWER TO the question as to how Francis had moved from Ditton to Stourhead is: by a circuitous route.

The only way I could follow Francis, in the absence of any other information, was to examine Henry the Magnificent's Ledger of Personal Accounts 1734–1749. There's a copy at Stourhead; the original is at the bank. This ledger was referred to as 'the Wilberry ledger'.[1]

It is in this ledger that we now see Francis's name appear for the first time. He's being paid for work done.

> 24th July 1736   Francis Faugoin The Gardener   £5 5s 0d

At this date Francis is twenty years old, not yet married and only a junior gardener. Two months later, on 28th September, Francis is given money to 'pay the labourers'; and on 4th October, is given ten guineas. The following year, Francis is given money every month to pay labourers totalling £125 0s 7d for January to December 1737.

We can presume from these payments that he was now in a position of regular employment with responsibilities for handling cash and managing the workforce.

The big problem with these entries is that they do not state at which property Francis was working. 'The Wilberry ledger' contains entries for Grateley, Quarley and Wilbury. The Hoares and the Bensons were friends all their lives, and their various properties were closely intertwined, hence the difficulty in interpreting the ledger and allocating payments correctly.

Another name now begins to crop up: Mary Swetman. Despite Jean's best efforts, a record of Mary's baptism has not yet come to light. There's an entry on 5th February 1736 for five guineas paid to Mary for 'Housekeeping', and on 8th March, six guineas. Her name appears in this ledger on several more occasions and continues for the next two years from January 1737 to December 1738. The last payment to her is for bills for housekeeping on 14th December 1738, 'in full to this day'.

It seems, therefore, that both Francis and Mary were employed, probably by Henry, at the same time, he as a gardener, she as a housekeeper. As far as we can tell, Francis was based at Grateley or Quarley, and Mary in London; she may have accompanied the family to Quarley, perhaps acting as nanny to the children while Henry pursued his favourite sport of fox hunting, as he kept hounds and horses there and went riding out with the local hunt. It is quite possible that Francis and Mary first met at Quarley, although we have no proof.

But we do have firm evidence for where and when they married.

On 26th January 1739, Francis and Mary married at the Church of St Mary Magdalene in Old Fish Street, London. He was twenty-three and she was twenty-two. The church was Anglican, not Huguenot. As we had discovered, Francis was described as a 'batchelor' of Grateley on the marriage register. We can be sure such a legal document confirmed he had to have lived in Grateley for him to be described thus. Mary was described as 'servant of this parish', that is, St Giles in the Fields. Henry's London house was in Lincoln's Inn Fields, in the same parish. At this date, Mary had been working for Henry at least two years and ten months, and Francis for almost two and a half years.

The ledger entry of 14th December 1738 is the last reference to Francis and Mary of which we can be sure. From then on, Francis and Mary's names disappear from the ledger. It is, perhaps, significant that this disappearance coincides with the years when Henry was away on the Grand Tour. He left England for the Continent in March 1739 (two months after Francis and Mary married) and returned in September 1741.

Putting on one side the mystery of the disappearance of Francis and Mary from the ledger, an entirely unexpected and fascinating piece of information came our way, which added to our knowledge of the Faugoin family.

Jean made an interesting discovery. She was Googling Francis Faugoin's name for the umpteenth time – and this time, something new came up: the sale particulars of a book. She immediately sent me the images, as she knew I would recognise its title: *The Complete Gard'ner or, Directions for Cultivating and Right Ordering of Fruit-Gardens and Kitchen-Gardens*, by Jean-Baptiste de la Quintinye, published posthumously in 1690.

Quintinye (1626–1688) initially trained as a lawyer but became Gardener-extraordinaire to Louis XIV at Versailles. He was responsible for creating the innovative Potager de Roi, the King's fruit and vegetable garden. He pioneered methods of cultivating sun-loving figs, melons and oranges in a northern climate, and growing strawberries out of season for the King's table. His garden can still be visited today, where there is a statue of him holding in his left hand a 'serpette', or grafting knife with a curved blade, and in his right hand graft material. He died at the home that Louis XIV had built for him, close to his beloved garden.

Quintinye's book was famous in its day. It was required reading for every gardener who aspired to showcase his skill in growing, training and producing immaculate fruit for the table of his wealthy employer. The book was first translated into English by John Evelyn (1620–1706), the writer, diarist, gardener and founder member of the Royal Society. As a Royalist, Evelyn fled England during the Civil War. He spent many years in France and married the daughter of the English Ambassador in Paris in 1647.

This edition of Quintinye's book, translated by Evelyn, is extremely valuable. Jean had discovered that it had been offered for sale in March 2015 by a New York saleroom, Swann Galleries. The price: US$2,250.

The particulars of the sale stated that the name of Francis Faugoin was on the paste-down as the owner, together with the date 1736 – the very year when Francis's name is first mentioned in 'the Wilberry ledger'. Of course, this could have been another Francis Faugoin, but we were confident it was him: a small inscription, in handwriting on the top right-hand corner, gave the name of Charles le Cerf and the date 1707.

Le Cerf was Francis's uncle – his mother's brother – and it was unlikely that anyone else would have known this fact, except perhaps for a descendant. In 1707, Charles would have been a young man of twenty-eight.

Suddenly, exciting possibilities opened up. Did Charles work at Versailles? Was the buyer a descendant of Francis? Would we be able to contact the buyer and learn the answers to all our questions and unsolved mysteries? Who else would be interested in buying such an expensive book? Maybe an institution or library? Or a collector of anti-quarian books with an interest in Quintinye?

I immediately emailed the saleroom, explaining that I was a researcher for the National Trust at Stourhead and that I was interested in the name Francis Faugoin. I also sent photos of his grave and the church. They replied very quickly and said they would forward my email to the buyer – but could not reveal the name.

We waited with bated breath. Nothing. We were bitterly disappointed.

Throughout our investigations into the life of Francis, we benefitted greatly from discussions with Dudley Dodd, who had been introduced to me by Alan Power. Dudley had retired from his position as Deputy Historic Buildings Secretary for the National Trust; he was a mine of information, which he generously shared with us. He has writ-ten many books and guidebooks on different aspects of Stourhead, and he took a keen interest in our progress. Jean and Dudley now urged me to try contacting Swann Galleries again.

A year after my first email, I got in touch with my contact there, Alexandra Nelson. I assured her that I was not a long-lost family member intending to turn up on the door-step. I hoped the buyer would be interested in finding out what I knew about Francis. Again, there was a speedy response from the gallery, but we were informed that the buyer had requested their name be withheld. I even asked if the gallery would be willing to act as a third party. Alexandra said she loved the photos of the church and very much hoped she might visit Stourhead one day. Naturally, I invited her to get in touch with me – and promised that I would give her a personal guided tour!

At the time of writing, we have not received any further information. Such are the disappointments and frustrations of research.

However, we were able to learn a lot from the information we had. Charles le Cerf was probably a favourite uncle; although married, he had no children and his will[2] revealed that he left money to all his numerous nephews and nieces. Charles had three sisters and one brother; between them, they had nineteen children. All were mentioned in his will, some receiving money to pay for apprenticeships. John and Susannah

Faugoin paid him the honour of naming their firstborn, Charles, after him. The will is dated 18th August 1733, two years before Charles le Cerf died in Wandsworth on 1st June 1735; his wife had died two months before him on 30th March. The will was made jointly with his wife, born Martha le Troyel, and stated that she had 'no relations in Great Britain and none that she knows elsewhere'. It was translated from French.

It's entirely possible that Charles worked in the gardens at Versailles during the latter years of the reign of Louis XIV (1638–1715). In the seventeenth and eighteenth centuries, the French were pre-eminent in the art of training fruit, achieving elaborate shapes – spheres, latticework, obelisks – all set in decorative and beautiful walled gardens. Quintinye's book was the most authoritative and up-to-date manual on the subject. As the will does not specify individual items, we can only imagine that it was given to Francis, as a fellow gardener, after the death of his uncle, and became a treasured possession. Was Francis a favourite nephew? Did the gift perhaps mark the occasion of Francis embarking on a promising career working for a successful and wealthy banker?

The more we learnt, the more mysteries we uncovered. And still we had no idea why Francis and Mary disappeared from 'the Wilberry ledger'. Where did they go?

1 Henry Hoare Ledger of Personal Accounts 1734–1749. C. Hoare & Co. archive: HFM/9/1.

2 Charles le Cerf will, 1735. TNA: PROB 11/671/451.

CHAPTER NINE

THE WEST COULSTON STORY

TRACKING DOWN FRANCIS was proving to be a stop-start exercise. Researching his life was rather like doing a jigsaw without being able to see the whole picture; and several important pieces were missing, perhaps lost for ever.

Then, suddenly one of the pieces popped up, in a random way. When Jean was looking through her notes on the baptisms of Francis and Mary's children – they had three boys – she noticed that two of the boys, Henry and Felix, were baptised at West Coulston. Although she had had this information for quite some time and had looked at it many times before, a thought suddenly occurred to her. Why were these baptisms in West Coulston, when their last child, John, was baptised in Stourton?

The realisation that Francis and Mary had two of their children baptised in West Coulston led to only one conclusion: they must have lived there.

We'd never heard of West Coulston and had no idea where it was. It is, in fact, just beyond Westbury near Edington, still in Wiltshire, and today about an hour's drive from Stourhead. Jean decided to go and find it and take a look round. She came back very excited: she was able to go into the church and stand by the font where Henry was baptised in November 1743 and Felix in July 1746. The rectors of Coulston listed for those dates were James Meredith (1738) and William Flower (1746). I was equally excited by this news and keen to go back with her to see if we could find any other information.

Jean also discovered that Coulston House – now known as Baynton House – was the home of William Godolphin. The name 'Godolphin' immediately rang bells with us. The 'Wilberry ledger' contained some puzzling entries, one of which, dated 19th May 1744, documented: 'By Mary Faugoin as given Her £1 16s od and to Mr. Godolphin's servants £2 2s od. Total £3 18s od'. Why was Henry giving a gratuity to Mr. Godolphin's servants? We had pored over this ledger entry discussing various scenarios, but with so little to go on it had remained a mystery – until now.

Could the reference to 'Mr. Godolphin's servants' imply also that Francis and Mary were employed by William Godolphin, and living at Coulston House or nearby?

On her first visit, the postman had told Jean where to find Baynton House, but she couldn't quite reconcile the geographical layout. This time, we bumped into a helpful resident who (probably suspicious of these two people snooping around) asked us what we were doing. She quickly put us right about the house we were looking for. We set out to find it, walking up the hill by the side of the church, then taking a footpath through some trees, coming out at the top of the drive leading down to the house. We walked a little way down the drive and were astonished to see a lovely garden coming into view.

A later owner of Baynton House commented that he thought the garden had many similarities with Stourhead, albeit on a much smaller scale. We could see what he meant. A small lake was surrounded by smooth grassy banks, a gunnera patch, a weeping willow by the edge of the water, and many large, well-established trees crowning the top of the opposite slope. We were astounded and delighted in equal measure by the picture in front of us. Nevertheless, however many similarities there appeared to be with Stourhead, we cannot deduce anything from these observations.

In 1742, the ledger records 'Mary Faugoin for Fruit Trees sent to Stourhead – £16 0s 0d'. We could never understand why she was sending fruit trees *to* Stourhead if she was already living there. Now, of course, we understood that she was living at West Coulston.

Four months after Henry's wife, Susan, died, Henry sent his daughter Nanny (Anne), aged six, to live with Mary, who was expecting her first child. On 6th January 1744, Henry paid Mary in full for '15 weeks board of Nanny by 23rd December and all disbursements'. An additional entry on the same date suggests that Henry had given his two older children two guineas each for the christening of little Henry Faugoin: 'By ditto for Harry and Sukey for her child's christening – £4 4s 0d'. Maybe Harry and Sukey (Henry Junior and Susanna) attended the christening, together with little Nanny (who was still living at West Coulston), or maybe they just bought a present for him.

So, Mary and Francis looked after Henry's precious younger daughter soon after the death of her mother. This was evidently a close family relationship. Henry must have greatly trusted Mary, who had known Nanny ever since she was born. The first reference to Mary in the accounts of February 1736 indicates that, aged nineteen, she was working for the Hoare family for more than a year before Nanny was born. At that time Henry was six, Susanna four and Colt, his younger son, only three. Mary had known all the children since they were little. Perhaps, at this time of sadness, Nanny wanted to be with someone who was a familiar and comforting face. I like to think that perhaps Mary was also a fun-loving character, just the person to help a little girl of six come to terms with the loss of her mother. Mary must have been very fond of the children, and they must have been fond of her. On 19th May 1744, Henry made the last payment to Mary for looking after Nanny: 'By Mary Faugoin in full of all demands for Nanny £12 13s 9d'.

It seems that Francis and Mary lived at West Coulston for about eight years. Why did they move there? It doesn't seem credible that Henry wished to terminate their employment, as otherwise he would never have sent his six-year-old daughter to stay with them at such a traumatic time. He also maintained a good relationship with them, giving his older children pocket money to spend at the christening of their first child. The only clues are the reference to the Godolphin servants and the fact that two of their children were christened in St Andrews Church, West Coulston. If we were correct in our assumptions about William Godolphin, what do we know about him?

William Godolphin inherited Coulston House in 1726 on the death of his aunt, Elizabeth Godolphin, who founded the Godolphin School in Salisbury. As a young child, William had suffered a traumatic event when his father, Francis Godolphin, committed suicide. He remained a bachelor and lived out his long life in the quiet Wiltshire village of West Coulston.

Did Henry suggest that Francis and Mary went to West Coulson to work for William Godolphin as gardener and housekeeper while he was away on the Continent visiting France and Italy?

There's another, somewhat tenuous, connection to the Godolphins. Francis Godolphin was the owner of the famous line of Arabian horses, which became known as the Godolphin Arabians. The stallion, Cade, was bred by Lord Godolphin and descended from one of the original three Arabians who were the 'fathers' of the thoroughbred racehorse. Cade had a respectable racing career but was more successful at stud, being Champion Sire in England between 1752 and 1769. His many valuable offspring included Miss Cade, born 1750. Miss Cade was given to Henry by his son-in-law, Lord Bruce, in April 1765. He mentions her frequently in his letters: 'I have just returned from a delicious ride which you have bestow'd on me with that Sweet pretty Mair,' he writes in one letter, going on to thank him for 'this so precious a present'. Knowing Henry's love and knowledge of horses, the gift of a mare sired by a famous racehorse from the Godolphin stables would, indeed, have been precious.

Knowing nothing about thoroughbred racehorses, I wanted to be sure that the name 'Miss Cade' was not given to more than one horse. Luckily, I knew just the person to ask. Judy Phillips is a volunteer at Stourhead; she owns and rides an Arabian and is a past President of the Arabian Horse Society. She confirmed that, indeed, there appeared to be two Miss Cades, both descended from the Godolphin Arabian. One mare was a chestnut and the other a bay. Unfortunately, Henry never mentioned the colour of *his* Miss Cade.

We also know that William Godolphin opened an account at Hoare's Bank in May 1779, which was closed by his administrators in October 1781.

The problem with all this is that the only mention of Godolphin that might relate to Francis and Mary Faugoin is the brief reference to paying a gratuity to his servants. This could be a red herring leading us down the wrong path entirely, and of no use at all in establishing who was employing Francis, and where he and Mary were living at the time.

However, there is another possibility. A wealthy banker, Peter Delmé (1710–1770) lived at Erlestoke, a village just over a mile from West Coulston. His father had been Lord Mayor of London and a Governor of the Bank of England. He was a patron of the arts and had an extensive collection of art in his London home at Grosvenor Square. He was an MP at the same time as Henry, and an acknowledged expert on horses.

It would seem, therefore, that there were more reasons for Francis to work for Delmé than for Godolphin. Godolphin's house and Delmé's house are within walking distance of each other, as shown on the Andrews & Dury map of 1773. So, given that there were two gardens belonging to wealthy men in the area, perhaps Henry 'loaned' Francis out to work for one, or both, of them.

This idea of Francis being 'loaned' to another employer to work in his garden had already occurred to me when thinking about the career of aspiring head gardeners. Young boys entering the profession of gardening would have followed a well-trodden path. In 1606, James I established gardening as a recognised profession when he incorporated by Royal Charter the Worshipful Company of Gardeners of London. One of the guild's first tasks was the instigation of a seven-year apprenticeship: applicants had to have had a good, basic education and were expected to pay a fee.

An apprentice gardener started his training on the bottom rung of the ladder. He was expected to carry out the most menial and repetitive tasks: weeding, hoeing, digging, raking paths, washing pots, lifting and carting manure for the hotbeds and greenhouses. A young gardener would have learned all he needed to know under the guiding eye of an experienced head gardener, and the patronage of a wealthy garden owner who did not need to look too closely at the wages bill. He also spent time working in different areas of the garden so that he gained knowledge of the management of the garden, and horticultural terms and practices.

Apprentices worked long hours. Sunday was their only day off. Most lived in the 'bothy', a small lean-to built on the north side of the north wall of the kitchen garden. The accommodation was basic. Although conditions varied, most were dark, damp and cold, with very little furniture.

Having completed their apprenticeship, the next step up the ladder was to become a 'journeyman' gardener. As the name implies, this involved moving from job to job, applying for positions in different parts of the country to gain as broad a range of experiences as possible; working his way from apprentice to journeyman, a gardener learned on the job. His next step was to apply for a position as a foreman or assistant head gardener. These appointments often came about through recommendation, either by the head gardener, or the owner of the establishment himself. Finally, the coveted role of head gardener could be achieved when young men reached their late twenties, after a long road of hard work and commitment. Only then could they consider getting married; apprentices were forbidden to marry.

Even the great Lancelot 'Capability' Brown (1716–1783) – the same age as Francis – followed this path. At the age of sixteen, he began working on his local estate of Kirkharle, in Northumberland, for Sir William Loraine. Having completed his apprenticeship there, he headed south and took up an appointment at Stowe, in Buckinghamshire, at the age of twenty-four, working for Lord Cobham for the next ten years. During his time at Stowe, Cobham gave him the opportunity of designing gardens for family and friends and effectively 'loaned out' his head gardener, enjoying the reflected glory. Following Cobham's death, Brown left Stowe in 1751 and established his own design office in Hammersmith, London. He spent the rest of his life designing gardens for wealthy, aristocratic clients, achieving fame and fortune.

A fortunate few took a slightly different career path. In some cases, young men came from a much-respected gardening family and had the craft of gardening in their blood. If they were lucky, their father was head gardener for a titled employer.

Francis was one of these. As we know, John, 2nd Duke of Montagu employed Francis's father at Ditton House. Francis didn't need to become an apprentice in the usual way; he'd been apprenticed to his father from an early age. When he was only twelve years old, he earned ten pence a day working from March to June for forty-five days. He had almost certainly spent his summer holidays and weekends working in his father's garden as a hands-on gardener. He had the added advantage of being given personal tuition by his knowledgeable father, not to mention a more comfortable existence than enduring the rigours of the bothy.

He did, however, have to secure further experience elsewhere as a 'journeyman gardener'. To further his career, he would need to move away from Ditton Park.

This recognised route for ambitious young men might explain the set of circumstances we had long tried hard to understand. After his apprenticeship under his father at Ditton, perhaps Duke John recommended Francis to Henry Hoare as a talented young gardener. Henry then employed him in the gardens at Quarley and Grateley. As Henry was planning an extended trip on the Continent, perhaps he decided to secure an appointment for Francis in another garden while he was away. Was this, perhaps, at Coulston House, working for William Godolphin, or at Erlestoke with Peter Delmé? The move would provide an opportunity for Francis to hone his skills and gain wider experience. He would then have reached the stage in his career when he could apply for the position of head gardener.

All this is merely a theory. And, in the absence of hard evidence, it must remain so. But at least it provides a plausible framework for what may have happened. We have tried time and again to solve this puzzle, following up every lead and the smallest snippet of information, but to no avail. Information will be out there, and new information constantly comes to light, but as yet we've been unable to find it. Our frustration is keenly felt, however. This time, we've come up against a brick wall. A wall of silence.

CHAPTER TEN

THE MISSING YEARS

❧

HERE FOLLOW EIGHT years of total silence from Francis before we hear from him again. But, if these years are unknown to us, life continued for Francis and Henry.

Although Francis is temporarily silent during these years, Henry is not. He had much to occupy him, and much to enjoy. The time was right for taking the Grand Tour. He left for the Continent in March 1739 and returned in September 1741. He was thirty-four, married with a young family. Unlike most young men embarking on the Grand Tour intent on having a good time, Henry planned this trip with a serious purpose. He'd read and studied so much about art that he wanted to see for himself the treasures Italy offered. At this date, there were no public galleries; all great art in this country was in the hands of private collectors. If you wanted to see paintings, sculpture, and architecture, then a visit to Italy and France was a must.

Henry set out from England with a manservant in early March 1739. They headed for Paris, then travelled south to Marseille and by boat to Genoa. By June, he had reached Venice. Travelling south again, he reached Florence by August 1739 and travelled on to Rome. By October that year, he'd returned to France to meet his wife at Aix-en-Provence, where they stayed for possibly a year. Susan Hoare returned to England in June 1741.[1]

> With an enlightened mind, the natural scenery of Italy attracted his notice
> and the study of the fine arts occupied that attention abroad, which the pursuit
> of the fox had hitherto done at home.[2]

This pithy and amusing comment was made by Richard Colt Hoare, Henry's grandson, when recalling Henry's words.

Henry's 'study of the fine arts' had begun well before he embarked on his tour of Italy. His 'enlightened mind' was evidently first encouraged by his uncle, William Benson. Benson had an extensive library. His love for architecture and literature – particularly Virgil and Milton – must have made a considerable impression on the younger Henry. To this young man, I think, Benson must have seemed a cosmopolitan figure, one who took an interest in intellectual and artistic pursuits – all of which would have been rather more appealing than the daily grind of business. It is thought that Benson may have later introduced Henry to the artist John Wootton, as well as the sculptor Michael Rysbrack and the architect, Henry Flitcroft, both of whom were to play a major role in the creation of the garden at Stourhead. Benson also commissioned Rysbrack to carve two busts of Milton, one as a young man and one in later life, and these can be seen in the Library at Stourhead. His son, Harry Benson Earle, and grandson, William Benson Earle, were frequent visitors to Stourhead, enjoying hospitality in good company.

John Wootton (1686–1764) specialised in horses and hunting scenes, and in his day was considered the foremost artist in this style. Three of his equine paintings hang in Stourhead house. His work was much sought after by the aristocracy, and George II commissioned a painting. Wootton also developed his own style of landscape painting, based on the work of Gaspard Dughet. If an original Dughet was beyond the means of a collector, then a good variation by a reputable artist was the next best thing. Henry bought several landscape paintings from Wootton, and they were on good terms.

Michael Rysbrack (1694–1770) was a Flemish sculptor and the son of a landscape painter. He arrived in London in 1720 and quickly established himself as one of the top three sculptors in the city, the other two being Roubiliac and Scheemakers. Skilled and confident, Rysbrack achieved almost instant success and was highly sought after.

Henry Flitcroft (1697–1769) was a talented English architect. He became Deputy Surveyor and Master Mason at the Office of Works, eventually being promoted to the role of Comptroller of the King's Works, a prestigious position at the top of the architectural field. He carried out many major commissions. From 1746 to 1756, he was Surveyor of the Fabric of St Paul's Cathedral, the first person to hold this position being Sir Christopher Wren.

These three artists ranked amongst the top exponents in their field and Henry patronised them all over a long period of time. He benefitted from their company and gained insights into how they worked. Henry recognised talent and rewarded it with friendship and loyalty. That loyalty did not go unnoticed. Rysbrack wrote to Henry on 19th May 1764, asking to be allowed to draw something of Henry's own choosing, '... which will give me the greatest pleasure in the world'. He also bequeathed the small terracotta model of Hercules to Henry in his will. Henry saw this model in Rysbrack's studio and commissioned Rysbrack to make a larger-than-life-sized statue in marble. This statue is in the Pantheon, and the terracotta model is on the desk in the Library.

In preparation for his trip to the Continent, Henry had French lessons in England. He spoke French, but not Italian. Just before leaving, an entry in the ledger dated 3rd March 1739 reads, 'Paid to Mons. Le Beau Pin for teaching me French – £3 3s 0d'. And on 4th March, 'Carried the balance to France – £20 18s 9d'. His books included the writings of Voltaire, and he owned sixteen French titles. Perhaps he was able to practise his French conversation with Francis.

There may have been an additional reason for Henry's visit to Italy, hinted at by Colt Hoare:

> The early part of his life was chiefly spent at Quarley in the society of many gay and fashionable young men who were fond of hunting and sacrificed rather freely to the shrine of Bacchus. But this gay and festive style of life did not continue long. Some of his young associates died and he found his own health so declining that (to use his own words) he was obliged to fly.[3]

This is corroborated by two newspaper entries. In *The London Evening Post*, 3rd–6th March 1739: 'Henry Hoare Esq. being in a Consumption is set out for the South of France by the advice of his Physicians.' And in the *Country Journal*, 13th October 1739: 'We hear that Henry Hoare Esq. Member of Parliament for Sarum who has been abroad for some time for the Recovery of his health intends to stay at Naples till next Summer. His Lady is gone over to him.' On Henry's return to England in the autumn of 1741, the *Daily Gazetteer* published the news: 'Henry Hoare Esq. the Banker and late a Member of Parliament for Salisbury who has been for a Year or more in the South Parts of France for his Health is returned to England with a very good Share of it and is since gone to his Seat at Quarley in Hampshire.'

To finance the trip, Henry made use of bankers and contacts along the way. In Italy, he used the services of Belloni, 'the greatest banker of all Italy', and in France, Sir John Lambert provided cash. In Florence, he met Sir Horace Mann, Envoy Extraordinary, who helped him negotiate purchases of art.[4] Seventeen years after returning from Italy, Mann was still acquiring paintings for Henry; in 1758, Mann bought two Gaspard Dughet landscapes for him from the Arnaldi family in Florence. Today, these hang in the Picture Gallery.

Many of the private residences in Rome were open to Grand Tourists. In the courtyard of the Palazzo Farnese, Henry would have admired the statues of Hercules and Flora. He would almost certainly have visited the Palazzo Doria Pamphilj, which housed a large private art collection, including two landscapes by Claude Lorrain.

Following in Henry's footsteps, Anne and I took our own 'Grand Tour' of Rome and visited the Doria Pamphilj to see the Claudes. Sadly, I could only acquire two postcards!

It is not difficult to understand the appeal to Henry and Susan of a long stay in Aix-en-Provence. Aix is a spa town situated in southern France, which afforded the opportunity of 'taking the waters', surely a more attractive proposition than chilly Bath. It enjoyed a balmy climate and breathtaking scenery: Mont Sainte-Victoire overlooks the medieval town.

The highlight of the entire two years, however, may well have been the purchase of 'The Pope's Cabinet' from a convent in Rome. The cabinet had originally belonged to Pope Sixtus V (1521–1590) but had been bequeathed to the convent by a nun who was the last surviving member of the Pope's family, the Perettis. Henry bought it around 1740. No records exist of what he paid for it, and he never revealed this information.

It is a magnificent work of intricate design and superb craftsmanship. The cabinet

The restored Pope's Cabinet in the Cabinet Room at Stourhead, Wiltshire | © National Trust Images/James Dobson
The cabinet was originally designed as a miniature church for Pope Sixtus V between 1585 and 1590, and was later acquired in Rome by Henry Hoare during his grand tour.

itself is over two metres tall and is mounted on a specially designed pedestal of mahogany, decorated with carved, gilded figures, giving an overall height of more than three metres. Built originally to house an organ, the interior consists of a complex assembly of small drawers faced in ebony, inlaid with ivory and with small ivory knobs. These would have been used to store small cameos, miniatures, jewels and curiosities.

But the cabinet's main glory is its exterior.

The façade was designed to resemble the façade of a Roman church, rising storey by storey to a pinnacle crowned with a carved and gilded statue. The entire front of the cabinet is covered by pietre dure – literally 'hard stones' – which is the craft of fitting together shaped and polished hard stones, semi-precious and precious gems in a decorative pattern. The stones were set in silver panels, fixed to the timber façade. The whole ensemble was then repeated many times to build up the complex design. The gems included lapis lazuli, amethyst, carnelian, garnet, mother-of-pearl, emerald, agate and coral.

It is impossible to over-emphasise the sensation it caused when visitors first saw it. It was commented upon by Jonas Hanway in his *Journal of Eight Days Journey from Portsmouth to Kingston upon Thames*, published in 1756.[5] Hanway was a celebrated traveller and philanthropist. He was the founder of the Marine Society and a governor of the Foundling Hospital, which provided a home in London for abandoned and orphaned children. He stayed several days at Stourhead as Henry's guest and said, 'the whole is a great curiosity and of high value'. High praise indeed from someone who must have seen many treasures on his travels through Russia and Persia. Horace Walpole, son of the Prime Minister, Robert Walpole, visited in 1762. Walpole was never effusive and only commented on things he deemed worthy of his attention, so his praise only serves to emphasise the cabinet's importance: 'A magnificent Cabinet, inlaid with precious Stones which formerly was an organ belonging to Sixtus Quintus'.[6] Mrs. Lybbe Powys, the socialite and diarist, visited in 1776. Her comments are in her usual gossipy style:

> In the third room shown us, is the so much talked on Cabinet that once belong'd
> to Pope Sixtus V, which Mr. Hoare purchas'd at an immense price, so great that
> he says he never will declare ye sum. It is indeed most Beautifully Ornamented,
> as well as valuable, for on the outside are many fine Jems ...[7]

The rich aristocrats who visited Italy on the Grand Tour were obsessed with pietre dure. Many examples of pietre dure boxes and caskets can be seen in their grand houses. Henry also bought other examples of pietre dure, such as small Florentine boxes to display in the house. But it is, without a doubt, the Pope's cabinet from Rome that is the main attraction. He must have been full of excitement when the purchase was completed and eagerly awaited its arrival at Stourhead.

Henry placed the cabinet, flanked by pillars, in what is now the Little Dining Room. Its huge size, sheer opulence, exquisite craftsmanship and colourful rare stones and jewels made the cabinet the main object of attention and speculation by visitors. It was always intended to impress and amaze and was never seen as a practical object.

It's easy to imagine how it would shimmer and glow in candlelight. Although maybe not to our taste today – perhaps too ostentatious and extravagant – there's no denying the craftsmanship: cabinet making, pietre dure, bronze casting, chasing and gilding, silversmithing and engraving on ivory. The use of rare and beautiful materials would have been appreciated and enjoyed by a contemporary audience. Although not visible, the interior is just as impressive, involving meticulous carpentry skills, and the use of ebony and ivory.

The presence of The Pope's Cabinet at Stourhead established Henry Hoare's reputation as a serious connoisseur and art collector. Today, the cabinet stands in its own niche in the Cabinet Room, against a suitably rich crimson background.

It is something of a miracle that the cabinet has survived. It endured a chequered career from the palace of a Pope in Rome in the 16th century to the home of an 18th-century banker in England; along the way it escaped the 1883 heirloom sale and the 1902 fire in the house. The National Trust undertook the mammoth task of carefully restoring this unique treasure, which was carried out in a specially constructed sealed, temperature-controlled workshop in the Column Room. Windows into this space allowed the public to see the conservator, Colin Piper, at work. The conservation work lasted more than a year and was completed in 2008 at a cost of £51,000.

So, Henry's Grand Tour had proved to be a success and a very enjoyable respite from his duties at the bank. He returned in good spirits and good health. But how these years were experienced by Francis, we have no idea. However, when they met again, it was to begin what turned out to be their life's work and legacy. What do we know about their personalities and the relationship they forged?

1 Jervis, Simon and Dodd, Dudley. *Roman Splendour English Arcadia: The English Taste for Pietre Dure and the Sixtus Cabinet at Stourhead*. National Trust. Philip Wilson Publishers, London, 2015. p. 132.

2 Hoare, Sir Richard Colt, Bt. *Pedigrees and Memoirs of the Families of Hore* Bath, 1819. p. 26.

3 Ibid.

4 Jervis, Simon and Dodd, Dudley. *Roman Splendour English Arcadia: The English Taste for Pietre Dure and the Sixtus Cabinet at Stourhead*. p. 132.

5 Hanway, Jonas. *A Journal of Eight Days Journey from Portsmouth to Kingston Upon Thames ... in a Series of Sixty-four Letters: Addressed to Two Ladies of the Partie ... By a Gentleman of the Partie*. London, 1756.

6 Walpole, Horace. *Journal of Visits to Country Seats &c.* Volume XVI, 1927–28. Ed. Paget Toynbee. The Walpole Society, Oxford, 1928. 'XXVI Journey to Stourhead, Redlynch, Longleate, Haselgrove, Melbury and Abbotsbury in July 1762'. pp. 41–44.

7 Climenson, Emily J., ed. *Passages from the Diaries of Mrs. Lybbe Powys (1776)*. Longmans, London, 1889.

Henry II Hoare on Horseback
MICHAEL DAHL (1656–1743) and JOHN WOOTTON (c.1682–1764)
Oil painting on canvas | 1726 | © National Trust Images

CHAPTER ELEVEN
PORTRAITS AND PROFILES

'FROM THE REGRET I feel in not knowing.' These words were written by Henry's grandson, Richard Colt Hoare, and have been echoed down the centuries by writers and historians striving to explain and interpret the garden at Stourhead.

My interpretation is a personal one, gained over many years, but it is still only a theory.

I see things from the perspective of Henry's character. It is a case of *'know me, know my garden'*. I've tried to understand the man, and in so doing, the garden has slowly revealed itself. Of course, we can never truly know the man; we can only attempt to comprehend his mindset against the backdrop of his time. We know the end of the story but can never know what it was like to know the beginning only.

Henry took ideas from various sources and re-interpreted them to reflect his personal life, thoughts and interests. Occasionally, he changed his mind. Henry was an astute and careful banker first and foremost, but he developed an appreciation of art and literature and possessed an enquiring mind and a good brain. He numbered artists and sculptors amongst his friends. He gained a reputation as a connoisseur. By looking at the evidence – the paintings he bought and commissioned, his letters, and what others said about him – we can perhaps begin to glean an understanding of Henry's character.

The first impressions are gained by looking at the portraits of him in the house.

Of the three portraits, two portray him on horseback. The first is the most striking: a large painting dominating the Entrance Hall. Henry commissioned this painting when he was twenty-one, the year he married his first wife, Anne Masham, and the year he became a Partner in the bank following the death of his father.

What does this portrait of Henry say about him? Only that he was wealthy and had enviable riding skills. Two artists were commissioned: Michael Dahl, a respected and admired Swedish artist, and John Wootton, the foremost sporting artist of the day. The portrait is signed by both artists and is dated 1726. Henry is wearing a fashionable blue silk riding coat over a gold embroidered red waistcoat, with black leather, thigh-high riding boots, and gold spurs and stirrups. His natural brown curls are shoulder-length. The ornate gold saddlecloth and gold accoutrements on the bridle are of the highest quality. Both horse and rider are looking straight at the viewer.

Henry is demonstrating his ability to ride 'The Great Horse', a term used in the 18th century to describe the agile but strong, muscular descendants of the Destriers, warhorses of the Middle Ages. Both forelegs are lifted off the ground and the horse is sitting back on its haunches. The pose depicted stems from the movements demonstrated by the Spanish Riding School in Vienna. It was one frequently chosen by men of influence and wealth. It reminded me of the equestrian bronze statue of Marcus Aurelius, Emperor of Rome; the original statue is now in the Capitoline Museum, but a replica can be seen outside in the Piazza.

A portrait of this kind was an unusual choice for a banker, compared with the solid, respectable images of his father and grandfather, depicting pride in their achievements. His father holds a drawing of his new Palladian mansion; his grandfather is portrayed wearing the fur-trimmed robes and regalia of Lord Mayor of London. Maybe they would not have approved of this portrayal of their successor from the next generation, who was expected to be a safe pair of hands in the senior position at the bank. Henry's portrait is of a dashing, wealthy young man, proud only of his ability to handle a spirited horse. There's a suggestion here of his youthful desire to show off – and this character trait is displayed in the garden; surely the Pantheon is the ultimate 'show-off' moment of the whole design? Knowing what we know of his later achievements, success and sadness, I find this an endearing quality. In this portrait, the future is before him.

The second painting portraying Henry, again on a horse, is in the Little Dining Room (opposite). This is also painted by Wootton, three years after the first portrait. I think this painting is much more realistic: it shows Henry, aged twenty-four, on a finely boned thoroughbred, together with his uncle Benjamin, enjoying his favourite pursuit of fox hunting. His groom and hounds are in the picture and Henry is indicating the way. The countryside spreads out behind them. This could easily have been at Quarley, where he kept a pack of hounds, or indeed in the Wiltshire countryside around Stourhead.

In common with many of his young friends, Henry enjoyed attending a well-organised and popular horse race in the nearby village of Mere. This race was similar to a modern point-to-point, and it involved serious money. T.H. Baker, a local historian, records that seven days before the race, the horses were paraded in front of The Ship Inn in Mere. Strict rules and regulations were issued, as follows:[1]

> Articles to be observed at the running for a Purse of 30 pounds on Mere Down
> on Monday, 3rd September 1733.
> ITEM – No horse, mare or gelding to start that hath ever won a King's Plate.
> ITEM – More than three horses must start for each plate.
> No subscriber to enter any horse but what is his own.
> No crossing, jostling or whipping allowed.

The course of the race was between Down Farm and Whitesheet Hill, and 'was patronised by all the leading Gentlemen in the County'.

The Meet of a Hunt with Henry II Hoare

JOHN WOOTTON (c.1682–1765)

Oil painting on canvas | 1729 | @ National Trust Images

Henry Hoare is mounted, wearing a grey coat, at the left and behind him a groom is leading up a second horse. The figure in the centre, standing beside his horse, elderly and wearing scarlet, may be the huntsman and behind him, at the right, Benjamin Hoare, in blue, mounted on a chestnut.

The 'leading Gentlemen' totalled thirty-four. They included the Right Hon. Thomas, Lord Weymouth from Longleat; the Right Hon. Thomas, Lord Stourton; the Right Hon. James, Earl of Castlehaven; the Hon. Samuel Masham Esq.; the Hon. Sir William Wyndham; Mr. Richard Hoare (Henry's younger brother); and, of course, Henry himself. Only Lord Weymouth and Henry placed bets of five guineas. Samuel Masham bet three guineas, Lord Stourton and Castlehaven one guinea each, and Richard Hoare two guineas. Most placed bets of one guinea. I'd love to know if Henry's horse was the winner, but sadly that wasn't recorded. I was interested to realise that amongst all his young friends, he remained on good terms with Lord Stourton (whose family were the previous owners of the Stourhead estate) and Samuel Masham, a schoolfriend from Westminster School and the elder brother of his first wife, Anne.

All his life, Henry took great pleasure in riding. He owned two Arabians. Miss Cade we've already met; the other was a stallion called Squirt. He loved them equally: 'The more I am acquainted with Squirt the more I admire Him. He is a sweet Fellow a safe Companion & an easy Friend.'[2] Henry commented that if he had his way, he would make him Secretary of State! After Squirt died, he mentioned them both in a letter: '... Miss Cade carryd me yesterday thro 3 hours rain and tho She is thought by the Jockeys too slight for me yet She is grown strong and left off cutting Daisies. I cannot mention Squirt without Tears in my Eyes ...'[3]

Henry's interests also included the country pursuit of 'shooting flying'. Colt Hoare later commented: 'he was a superior marksman, at a period when the art of shooting flying was but little known and practised'. 'Shooting flying' referred to shooting birds on the wing, rather than bagging them when they were on the ground. Until the late 17th century, birds were traditionally shot whilst on the ground or perched. With the improvement in shotgun technology in the early 18th century, birds began to be shot in flight. The term 'shooting flying' derived from the French '*tir au vol*'. This method of shooting game birds soon became more popular among the aristocracy and landed gentry than hawking or netting.

The third picture of Henry is a pastel drawing on paper, thought to have been made about 1765, when Henry would have been sixty (opposite). The artist, William Hoare of Bath RA (1707–1792) was not a relation but was a great friend of Henry's. As a young man, William had spent time in Italy learning his trade, specialising in portraits in oils and pastels. He returned to Britain to live in Bath and moved in the artistic circles there. He was a frequent guest at Stourhead; his daughter, Mary, married Henry's nephew 'Fat Harry'.

This drawing shows Henry in profile. He is wearing a grey wig tied back at the nape of the neck with a black silk bow, and sporting a vibrant blue coat, a gold embroidered waistcoat and a white neckerchief. His long straight nose is unmistakable and there's

just the hint of a double chin. We have the impression of a serious and respected man of business, one who has seen life and left his youthful exuberance behind. The original of this picture is held at the J. Paul Getty Museum in Los Angeles, but there is a copy at Stourhead in the Little Dining Room.

We have these three paintings of Henry showing him in youth and middle age. But what did Francis look like? Frustratingly, there are no official portraits of Francis. However, we can turn to Henry's friend, the artist Coplestone Warre Bampfylde. In 1775, he painted a view across the lake, with the Pantheon in the background. This picture hangs in the Library. The date of this painting is significant because it shows the finished garden. Two little dogs, sheep, and swans swimming on the lake animate the scene. And, in total, we can see sixteen people: two people are walking across the bridge and two more stand on the bridge, one of whom is fishing; two people are strolling along the footpath by the lake; another person further along the bank is also fishing; a party is enjoying boating on the lake. A coach travelling along Gasper Road can be seen in the distance, followed by two single figures on horseback. Two more riders are

Stourhead Pleasure Grounds, Wiltshire, View to the Pantheon (detail)

galloping down the hill from Top Wood. Henry must have commissioned this picture to show people enjoying his garden.

But, best of all, Bampfylde has placed three figures in the foreground. These figures, unlike all the others, are drawn in considerable detail.

One figure is sitting on a round wooden bench. This seated figure wears a blue silk suit and is hunched over, leaning on a stick, perhaps listening to the conversation between the other two people.

A second figure is standing, clearly giving instructions to a third person, who is also standing. As far as I know, no one has previously identified the central figure as Henry. However, I'm certain it is him, as he can surely be recognised: a tall, slim, well-dressed man with a distinctive profile. His grandson, Richard Colt, later described him as 'tall and comely in his person, elegant in his manner and address and well versed in polite literature'.[4] His left arm is raised, as if pointing out something. We can be certain Bampfylde would not have given such prominence, centre stage, to an ordinary visitor.

The third figure is also detailed. He is doffing his hat with a slight bow of deference and obviously listening to what is being said to him. I'd often looked at this picture until, one day, the significance of it dawned on me. I had long decided that Henry was in the picture, but this time I suddenly realised: the other figure could be Francis Faugoin. This was a eureka moment.

I thought of a way of testing out my theory. I decided to ask the National Trust Curator of Costume, Shelley Tobin, to comment on the clothes worn by the figures and what those clothes signified. I sent her a digital image of the painting, but closely cropped, only showing the figures, so there were no clues as to the location. This was her reply:

> 'HENRY' – he is wearing a red military inspired coat, ruffles at the cuffs,
> white silk stockings and elegant, buckled shoes. He is pointing to something
> in the landscape and obviously giving instructions. He is probably superior
> to the person to whom he is talking. He has not removed his hat.
>
> 'FRANCIS' – he is wearing a brown coat, probably woollen with a striped,
> blue silk waistcoat and strong leather shoes. He is bowing/listening to the
> person in the red coat. He has removed his hat.

As I didn't tell her anything about the two people, or the location, I thought this was an amazingly accurate description. I was interested to know that, although Francis was wearing workmanlike clothes, he sported a silk waistcoat. So, he's not a labourer. Shelley mentioned that the collection at Killerton, where she was based, contained a similar waistcoat. As Jean had already planned a meeting there, I joined her and went along to see it. The waistcoat was almost identical to the one in the painting.

So, in the absence of any portraits of Francis – thus far – I am happy to speculate that this is probably what he looked like.

Another intriguing aspect of this painting is its subject matter. At the time, it was fashionable for the owner of a large establishment to commission a painting portraying him seated in his garden, accompanied by his wife and children, and possibly pets: dogs and horses. These paintings became known as 'conversation pieces'. A painting by Arthur Devis, dated 1761, for example, shows Sir John Shaw in the park at Eltham Lodge, Kent, together with his wife and three young children with a pet whippet and a horse-drawn chaise.[5] Two Zoffany paintings of 1762 depict the great Shakespearean actor-manager, David Garrick, in his garden by the Thames at Hampton, Middlesex. One of the canvasses features a Temple dedicated to Shakespeare; Garrick and his wife are standing on the steps accompanied by a small King Charles spaniel; a large dog is lying on the grass in front of the Temple; Garrick, holding a cane, is indicating a third figure, who could be a gardener. The other painting shows Garrick and his wife entertaining a visitor to tea in the garden.

Henry clearly wanted a record of his finished masterpiece. But, unlike other 'conversation pieces', he chose to show ordinary people enjoying his garden. He also chose to include someone else of importance: his gardener, Francis Faugoin. In 1775, when this picture was painted, Henry was seventy and Francis fifty-nine; they had been working together at Stourhead for twenty-eight years. Did Henry want to indicate for posterity that this other person was partly responsible for the creation of this idyllic scene? Did he wish to acknowledge and celebrate Francis?

For further insights into Henry's character, we can turn to his correspondence with his son-in-law Lord Bruce who, in 1776, was elevated to an earldom, taking the title Lord Ailesbury. When I first read these letters, I was astonished by how informal they were, full of references to his family and amusing anecdotes. It struck me, even then, when I was just beginning my research, that his character comes shining out of the page.

Thanks go to Kenneth Woodbridge, the first modern historian to become interested in Stourhead, who, in the 1950s, tackled the mammoth task of transcribing the correspondence, which was typed up by his wife, Joan. In fact, these letters are all from Henry to Lord Bruce, beginning in 1760; Bruce's replies are now lost. Thanks also go to Dudley Dodd, who has gathered these letters together in one volume.[6] Dudley has painstakingly referenced everyone mentioned and given a detailed analysis of the main events. I'm also grateful that these letters are in the safe hands of the Wiltshire & Swindon History Centre archives and can be viewed there by anyone today. Nothing beats seeing the original marks on the page and a signature: knowing that those hands have touched, held, folded the paper, and stamped the seal into the hot, red wax. Henry's handwriting is the most personal thing we can see from his life – present, now, in our lives.

Henry lived and worked in London for a greater part of the year. After the death of his mother, he used Stourhead mainly in the summer months, and for entertaining. The house was much smaller then; the two wings housing the Library and the Picture Gallery, the curving drive and the clock tower were added later by Colt Hoare. There was a spacious lawn at the back of the house and a walled garden. The famous garden did not yet exist.

First and foremost, Henry was a competitive, shrewd and canny businessman. He was always ready to adopt new ideas. There are many quotes illustrating his strong work ethic and attention to the minutiae of business, which he made sure his family working alongside him never forgot. He drummed into them that the luxuries of life would not be available to them if they neglected the business: '... provided their foundations are laid by the hand of prudence and supported by perseverance in well doing and constant cautious watchfulness over the main chance'.[7] In 1755, he wrote to his nephew, Richard, 'whether at pleasure or business let us be in earnest and ever active to be outdone or exceeded by none, that is the way to thrive ...'. I think he may have inherited this drive and ambition from his grandfather, Sir Richard, who also urged hard work and an understanding of what it takes, not only to succeed, but to remain successful over a long period of time. Victoria Hutchings in her book, *Messrs. Hoare Bankers*, writes of Sir Richard: 'Throughout his career he displayed energy, determination and integrity, qualities which earned him a fine reputation and a profitable business which he took great pains to pass on to all his sons.'[8]

These were qualities his grandson clearly inherited. It's easy to forget that the creation of the garden at Stourhead was not Henry's only achievement; he had to pay close attention to the bank and indeed steer it through two wars: the Seven Years' War (1756–1763) and the War of American Independence (1775–1783). Not so very different, in fact, from our own times. He repeated, again and again, that the luxuries of life couldn't be fully appreciated unless they were earned by 'application to business'.

Henry may have been a stickler for hard work, but he certainly knew how to throw a party. And he had a delicious sense of humour. So many of his letters refer to the enjoyment of good company and good food, and he adored all his grandchildren. He was particularly fond of Harriot, his daughter Susanna's only child by her first marriage to Lord Dungarvan, referred to as 'Miss H.F.B' (Henrietta Frances Boyle).

> *6th July 1765*
> I hope the Moss Roses bring forth Thousand & Ten Thousands, in short, as many as We have Strawberrys here, 20 of each sort which I wish were in H.F.B.'s merry mouth with a piece of Ice Cream at the Heals of Them, that's all the harm I wish Her.[9]

Ice cream was one of the little luxuries enjoyed by the family; they were fortunate enough to have an ice-house in the top garden near the house. Of course, it was Francis who was responsible for producing twenty varieties of strawberries in the peak of perfection.

Henry always took pains to dress well and look his best on family occasions, another luxury he enjoyed. When writing to Lord Bruce five years later, Henry asks:

> *8th February 1770*
> ... I beg of Your Lordship to tell Miss H.F.B. that you saw me to day in my
> 8 spangle Button hole Coat & Waistcoat which I shall soon lay up in Lavender
> till the Xning of Her first Child.[10]

When Susanna's children by her second marriage, to Lord Bruce, began to grow up, Henry delighted in showing them round the garden.

> *11th May 1776*
> Thank God they are all fine & well & now make nothing of walking round
> the Gardens & I mounted The Tower Thursday with the Dear Children &
> They are vastly delighted with this spot.[11]

In another letter, Henry talks about Charles, who was the last son of Susanna and Lord Bruce and the baby of the family.

> *25th July 1774*
> I rejoyce to hear The Dear Children are so well & that the lovely Charles is
> trying to play on The organs of Speech. I wish I was within a Kiss of Him.[12]

This is such an endearing comment. Henry is not afraid to show his feelings. It's clear that, like any grandparent, he took pleasure in showing them his creation; he would be astonished, and surely delighted, to see how many children run around and play in his garden today.

Henry was a generous host and enjoyed entertaining friends and family. His grandson Richard Colt said, '... his hospitable table was ever open to friends, neighbours and strangers; and the artist was ever esteemed a welcome guest ...'. On one occasion, he had invited his Chief Clerk, the newly married Charles Wray, to a gathering. Another young couple, 'Fat Harry' and his new wife, Mary, were also at the party, spending their honeymoon at Stourhead. Fat Harry was Henry's nephew, and Henry was also his godfather. This is what he said:

> *6th July 1765*
> ... Brides & Bridegrooms arrive here dayly & grow up like Mushrooms.
> The Wrays are come & I begin to be afraid of opening a Door for fear of
> interrupting Their amorous Billing ...[13]

I laughed out loud when I first read this.

Fat Harry became known as a man-about-town and bon viveur. Harry and Mary enjoyed all that London society could offer: music, art and theatre. They lived at a smart address: Adelphi Terrace, behind the Strand. His next-door neighbour was none other than David Garrick. Fat Harry invited Garrick along to one of these sociable evenings at Stourhead, and Garrick entertained his host by composing an impromptu poem. Needless to say, Garrick held an account at the bank and there's a portrait of him there. When he retired, he sold his share in the Theatre Royal, Drury Lane and immediately walked round to Hoares to bank the cheque.

It is rather wonderful to know that this same spirit of hospitality is continued today. The Garrick Club members are occasionally entertained at Stourhead, enjoying champagne in the Grotto and good food in the Pantheon. Henry would have been delighted.

Making the garden at Stourhead must have given Henry another opportunity to create pleasure for guests. It provided relief from the pressures of work; it offered practical challenges and a lot of fun to be had along the way. He shared this sense of pleasure with family and friends – and with the wider public.

So, I think we can see why he was called 'Henry the Magnificent'. We don't know when this nickname began to be used, or who was the first person to use it. I like to think it was probably his close friends. Perhaps they were appealing to his sense of humour by affectionately poking fun at him, comparing him with Lorenzo the Magnificent: Lorenzo de Medici, Renaissance prince, banker and one of the most famous art patrons in history.

Meanwhile, what do we know of Francis's character? Because he came from a Huguenot family, we can be fairly certain he had a similar work ethic to Henry's. As refugees, the Huguenots knew what it took to persevere in the face of adversity.

Maybe Henry saw in Francis qualities that echoed his own youthful ambition. He offered Francis the opportunity of working for him at Quarley, and Francis quickly accepted the new responsibility. He clearly inherited from his father a sense of confidence, a good understanding of what it meant to work for a visionary employer, and perhaps a sense of ease when conversing with creative people. He must have been a strong character to satisfy Henry's demands for perfection. Throughout his life, Henry spotted and nurtured talent; a close working relationship must have existed between them.

And Francis must have been well paid. He was able to deposit money in an account held by Fat Harry at the bank, a separate account for the administration of short-term loans and annuities. In her 'Manuscript of the Month', Pamela Hunter, the archivist at Hoare's, says:

> These activities were confined for the most part to family, friends and other close connections. But the sums involved were considerable. In 1777, Harry calculated that he held over £57,500 on behalf of others ... including his uncle's Stourhead steward Francis Faugoin (£1,295) ... For some, depositing money with Harry was a convenience; their cash was earning a reliable income while remaining accessible at short notice. For others, it boiled down to trust.[14]

So, Francis was in a position to put money aside in a savings account. But money alone could not account for such a long, productive and creative partnership.

Although we do not have any official portraits of Francis, we do know where he lived: predictably, in the Gardener's House. Francis Nicholson painted a charming picture of this cottage, which was used on the cover of the 2002 National Trust guidebook. Francis Nicholson (1753–1844), known as the father of watercolour painting, was commissioned by Colt Hoare to paint views of the garden in 1813 and 1814. Colt Hoare inherited the house, garden, and estate in 1783, two years before Henry died. He was a good artist himself, and a keen collector of topographical paintings and drawings.

The cottage stood opposite the Bristol Cross. On this spot today stands the wooden kiosk that serves as the entrance into the garden. The cottage was thatched, with a dormer window in the centre of the roofline, projecting forwards over the entrance doorway beneath. The pretty porch and fence each side of the doorway were added later by Colt Hoare, long after the death of Francis. In Nicholson's picture, the Pantheon can be glimpsed in the distance; two people are walking across the dam and two more standing on the bridge, admiring the view. The path terminates at the cottage; a dense planting of trees and shrubs at the end of the path blocks the way. It was clearly not possible to walk on from this point into the garden, as can be done today. Colt Hoare added new paths round the lake at a later date, which then passed close to the Temple of Flora.

Colt Hoare kept a diary, referred to as 'the Annals', in which he recorded all the changes he made to the landscape and improvements he carried out:

> 1808 – The Gardener's House in the village new modelled.

Five years after 'new modelling' the cottage, he recorded:

> 1813 – In the spring of this year the Gardener's House was consumed by fire; it was one of the oldest houses in the parish and stood within the gardens facing the Bristol Cross. I had lately spent a good deal of money in decorating it and it became a pretty object – in the autumn I took down the materials and levelled the ground on which it stood.

Further evidence of the Faugoin family is in the church. There is a memorial tablet located high up over one of the arches in the north aisle as you enter the church. The tablet features a shield with a coat of arms, a motto and the names of the family. The motto reads 'Vincit qui Patitur' – 'He who endures will succeed' – a fitting motto for Huguenot refugees.

But the memorial tablet may also contain tantalising information about the status of the Faugoin family as gardeners, particularly in France. I hoped this information would

be revealed by understanding the meaning of the symbols on the coat of arms.

The coat of arms is divided into three horizontally. And the reason for these divisions was to show an alliance or occupation. In the centre is the fleur-de-lys with a lion above and below. In heraldic terms, the lions could be described as 'lion passant' – walking – facing left with the right forepaw raised. The lion symbolises courage, nobility or royalty.

The shield is surmounted by what appears to be a kind of pennant. On more careful examination it is possible that this 'pennant' could represent a serpette, which was a short knife with a curved blade. This tool was used by gardeners to graft one variety of plant to another variety. This technique is used extensively in the fruit garden.

We already knew that Francis owned a copy of Quintinye's book and, as stated earlier, there is a statue of Quintinye holding a serpette in the Potager du Roi at Versailles. Did the symbols on the shield give further evidence that there may have been a royal connection? Specifically, a connection with the cultivation of fruit in the garden at Versailles?

I tried many avenues of enquiry in this country before turning to France for an answer. A friend and fellow volunteer, Diane Ellis, teaches French and I asked if she would translate a letter for me. I have found that friends are always interested in Francis's story and are keen to help.

Close up of shield on Faugoin memorial | Photograph: Alan Barker

Diane discovered that, historically, families specialised in various trades (*métiers*) – stonemasons, sculptors, gardeners – and their occupations were represented by symbols on their shield (*blason*). On further investigation I discovered that there was a *blason de métier* specifically for vignerons (winemakers). This depicted a serpette flanked by bunches of grapes on the vine above a trellis. I also found that any *blason* with connections to Versailles always featured three fleur-de-lys. Did the shield on the memorial indicate that the Faugoin family worked for Louis XIV at Versailles, specialising in viticulture?

I drafted a letter explaining my interest in the Faugoin shield. Diane suggested that I send this to M. Jean-Jacques Lartigue, Président du Conseil Français d'Héraldique. Sadly, he replied informing me that there aren't any Faugoin family shields in the French armorial records.

All this is speculation. Once again, I've pursued many avenues to try to understand the symbolism of the shield, but to no avail.

The inscription on the memorial gives details of the whole family. The tablet was made by Chapmans of Frome. Joseph Chapman (1784–1853) was a successful local stone mason. This memorial may have been commissioned by a Faugoin family member or, possibly, by Colt Hoare. He paid for the gravestone of Jane Lloyd, the housekeeper, which lies next to the tomb of Francis.

We now had a most exciting breakthrough. Whilst looking through some documents at C. Hoare & Co., Dudley enquired if Pamela Hunter, the archivist, had ever come across any correspondence between Francis and Henry. It was a long shot but, to his delight, she produced a letter from Francis to Henry referring to the Watch Cottage. It was entirely due to Pamela's careful archiving of material and her extensive knowledge that the letter came to light. Dudley was not able to take a photo at the time, but he did send us an extract. We never expected to be lucky enough to find an original letter from Francis and to have the pleasure of seeing his handwriting. This was hugely important: finding an original letter revealed much valuable information. Dudley gave me the reference and we subsequently visited the Bank and saw the letter.[15] Pamela let me have a digital image showing the complete text and, of course, the all-important signature.

The letter was dated 2nd March 1782 and addressed to Henry at his London house in Clapham. This was only three years before Henry died; Francis was sixty-six. The first part of the letter informs Henry of 'the age of the trees in the vales'. Francis said, 'I have examined back my accounts and find the first planting of trees from Mount Pleasant to William Meads is twenty years since' and that 'they were some four and five years old when they were planted'. This gives us proof that Francis kept detailed accounts. Sadly, these accounts have never been found. In his letter, he goes on to say that the trees were 'stript up and thinned' and the resulting brushwood used to make faggots, which were taken to the brickyard to burn bricks.

He then turns his attention to the 'Cottage by the Pantheon', which today is called the Gothic Cottage, but was then referred to as Watch Cottage. Francis is asking for instructions about proposed improvements:

> I do not think we need be afraid of any more Frost, therefore have told White the Plaistere to begin lathing the Cottage by the Pantheon and to begin the first coat of Plaister – the covering of straw may also be taken from the new stone seat and the window glazed but don't know what sort of form you would have the glass, somewhat like those at the Convent.

The Convent was another small cottage, situated in the woods of the estate.

Francis's letter gives us a tiny window into his world. The weather had been cold, but the threat of frost had passed. He would like instructions on the design of the windows for the cottage before he can proceed with the glazing. He refers to the stone seat being 'new'. These were the kind of discussions he would have had with Henry on the day-to-day management of the garden. The gardeners today discuss the details of a work schedule in exactly the same way, and it's a telling reminder of the continuity of the care still taken all these years later. Francis Faugoin and Tim Parker, the present head gardener, would have a lot in common.

1 Baker T.H. *The Baker Volumes*. Volume I, pp. 117–118. Mere Library, Wiltshire County Libraries.

2 Dodd, Dudley, ed. *The Letters of Henry Hoare 1760–1781*. Wiltshire Record Society, Wiltshire & Swindon History Centre, Chippenham, 2018. p. 70. WSA 9/35/165(1)/2413.

3 Ibid. p. 104. WSA 9/35/165(1)/-.

4 Hoare, Sir Richard Colt, Bt. *Pedigrees and Memoirs of the Families of Hore*. Bath, 1819. pp. 28–29.

5 Felus, Kate. *The Secret Life of the Georgian Garden*. I.B. Tauris & Co. Ltd, London, 2016. p. 48, Fig. 13.

6 Dodd, Dudley, ed. *The Letters of Henry Hoare 1760–1781*. Wiltshire Record Society, 2018.

7 Hutchings, Victoria. *Messrs. Hoare Bankers. A History of the Hoare Banking Dynasty*. Constable & Robinson Ltd, London, 2005. p. 56.

8 Ibid. p. 8.

9 Dodd, Dudley, ed. *The Letters of Henry Hoare 1760–1781*. Wiltshire Record Society, 2018. p. 84. WSA 35/165(1)/14232.

10 Ibid. p. 122. WSA 1300/2878.

11 Ibid. p. 152. WSA 1300/2948.

12 Ibid. p. 138. WSA 9/35/165(2)/-.

13 Ibid. p. 84. WSA 35/165(1)/1423.

14 Hunter, Pamela, Manuscript of the Month, 2015. Fat Harry Account. C. Hoare & Co archive.

15 C. Hoare & Co archive: HFM/8/8.

CHAPTER TWELVE
THE GARDEN BEGINS

STOURHEAD HOUSE SITS in an ancient landscape. It faces east, looking out across a wide sweep of chalk downland, typical of Wiltshire. Seen from the front of the house, the long, flat-topped ridge known as Whitesheet Hill rises up to meet the vast expanse of sky. The view from the top is spectacular, and on a hot summer's day the scent of wild thyme fills the air. Chalk downland flowers have a fragile, ephemeral quality: harebells, scabious, the tiny blue flowers of chalk milkwort and common spotted orchids. The rare Adonis Blue butterfly thrives in this habitat, and skylarks rise ever higher with their piercing sweet song. Ancient woodland of beech, oak and yew threads through this landscape, remnants of the great forest of Selwood and the hunting forests of King John.

At the foot of Whitesheet Hill, the chalk uplands give way to a fertile greensand plateau. Farmland spreads out on this level ground, which then drops away steeply into the valleys to the south. Where the porous chalk meets the greensand, underground springs of crystal-clear water emerge onto the surface, becoming streams and rivers that carve out these hidden valleys. The River Stour rises at the head of one such valley, giving Stour Head its name.

Long before the house was built by the Hoares, long before this land was granted to Lord Stourton – in a time before memory – people made their mark on this place. Neolithic remains of a causewayed enclosure, dating from 3,000 bc, can be seen – if you know where to look. Bronze Age barrows and traces of an Iron Age hillfort are also visible. Stonehenge lies a few miles to the east.

Henry Hoare, too, made his mark.

The world-famous garden of Stourhead is enhanced by this ancient landscape. Colt Hoare acknowledged this by saying that the garden 'owes its greatest beauty' to 'abundant springs, the purest water, to the sun and surrounding woods, these grown old – nature has formed the outline and art has completed the picture'.

At some time in the distant past, the Stourton family dammed the river to form a chain of ponds. Henry's father, Good Henry, commissioned a map in 1722, which quite clearly shows this configuration: river, valley, ponds and dams. This map can be seen at the Wiltshire & Swindon History Centre.[1] The river flows down the valley, now known as Six Wells (referring to the six springs). Steeply wooded slopes are shown on each side of the river, which has been dammed in three places to create three small ponds. The valley floor then widens and flattens into pasture and meadow, and the river continues, flowing into three more ponds, the largest of which is a considerable size and is likely to have been a millpond serving the mill at a lower level.

This is the landscape Henry inherited after the death of his father. The garden and lake had not yet been created.

Henry began experimenting with garden design when he created the Fir Walk, high up on the hillside above the valley. This long straight avenue of grass, cropped close by sheep, was lined on each side by fir trees and was in place by 1733. This date is confirmed by a later article in the *The London Chronicle* of Thursday, 16th to Saturday, 18th June 1757.[2]

> On the brow of this hill is a walk of considerable extent of the softest, mossy turf, bordered on each side by stately Scotch Firs of Mr. Hoare's own planting, about twenty-four years since.

In the four years following 1733, Henry was to lose a daughter and gain a daughter. Anne, the daughter by his first wife Anne Masham, died in January 1735; Anne, his second daughter by Susan, his second wife, was born on 27th June 1737. Eighteen months later, in the early spring of 1739, Henry left for the continent.

Henry returned to Stourhead in the autumn of 1741 to start a new chapter in his life – a life without his young son Colt, who had died while he was away, in early May 1740. With Henry's help and advice, his mother, Jane, had made finishing touches to the house, turning the elegant mansion into a comfortable home, using money left in his father's will expressly for this purpose. Nine months after his return, in June 1742, Jane died. Although the date of her death is often quoted as June 1741, this is an error, as confirmed by the following entries in the newspapers.

> *Daily Post*, 15th June 1742
> Mrs Jane Hoare, who died last Week at Stourton, in Wilts, was Widow of the late Henry Hoare Esq, and Mother to Henry Hoare Esq, Member in the last Parliament for Salisbury, and to Mr Alderman Hoare ...

> *London and Country Journal*, 18th June 1742
> Last Week died at Stourton in Wilts, Mrs Hoare, (Relict of Henry Hoare Esq, formerly an eminent Banker in Fleet-street), Mother of Henry Hoare Esq, Member in the last Parliament for Salisbury; and of Alderman Hoare.
> By her Death ... and the fine seat at Stourton, comes to her eldest Son, Henry Hoare Esq.

Less than a year later, tragedy was to strike yet again. In May 1743, his much-loved wife, Susan, died. Henry was left a widower at the age of thirty-eight, with three young children to care for: Henry, aged thirteen; Susanna, eleven; and Anne, six. He never married again.

After such a devasting loss, Henry needed to fill the void. He remembered all he had seen in Rome: the temples and the statues. The first tentative steps were taken when he placed a small classical temple at the point where the Fir Walk met the walk from the statue of Apollo on the south lawn. This was called the Temple on the Terrace, also known as the Venetian Seat (a detailed description is given in Appendix II).

At the same time, he resolved to build another, more ambitious, temple, lower down the hillside. This he called the Temple of Ceres, and in it he placed a beautiful antique state of Ceres, the goddess of fertility, the harvest and motherhood.

There has been much debate amongst historians about the inscription over the door: 'Procul, O Procul, este Profani' ('Begone, begone, all ye who are uninitiated'). Some have suggested that it was intended to instruct visitors to enter the garden with respect and in a reverent frame of mind. However, there is an alternative view, which seems more plausible to me. In his article in the *Journal of Garden History*,[3] 'A Mistaken Iconography? Eighteenth-century Visitor Accounts of Stourhead', Dr Oliver Cox suggested that the Temple of Ceres was a dedication to Susan, and that the quotation was a specific instruction to enter this specific temple with respect for her. The Roman architect and engineer Vitruvius specified temples to Ceres be placed in rural surroundings to which the public are not necessarily led, other than for the purpose of making sacrifices to her. 'This spot is to be reverenced with religious awe and solemnity of demeanour by those whose affairs lead them to visit it.' Henry's temple, too, was hidden away amongst the trees, long before the lake was in place. It was the last thing visitors would see, not the first. The path in front of the Temple was placed there much later by Colt Hoare when he made changes to the garden. Colt Hoare made this clear when he commented that the view of the lake and the Pantheon was:

> ... indeed the very best and most picturesque which the gardens can afford,
> and therefore should be seen the last and form the finale of this promenade –
> it frequently however is seen the first whenever company visit the gardens
> from the Inn; on which account we recommend the starting from the house
> and not the inn.[4]

Furthermore, in 1745, when the Temple was completed, it was not possible to walk on into the garden, because the garden did not yet exist. This inscription remains the subject of debate.

When out on his early morning gallop along Terrace Ride, perhaps Henry had looked down and seen the sun glinting on the water of the ponds far below in the valley. In the hot summer of 1765, he wrote to Lord Bruce:

> Next I ride under the spreading Beaches just beyond the Obelisk on the Terrace
> where We are sure of Wind & Shade & a delightfull View into the Vale ...[5]

This effect may have reminded him of Lake Nemi, a small, circular lake south of Rome, formed in the crater of an old volcano. The steeply wooded slopes surrounding the crater rise up to the town of Nemi, placed high on the hilltop looking down on the lake.

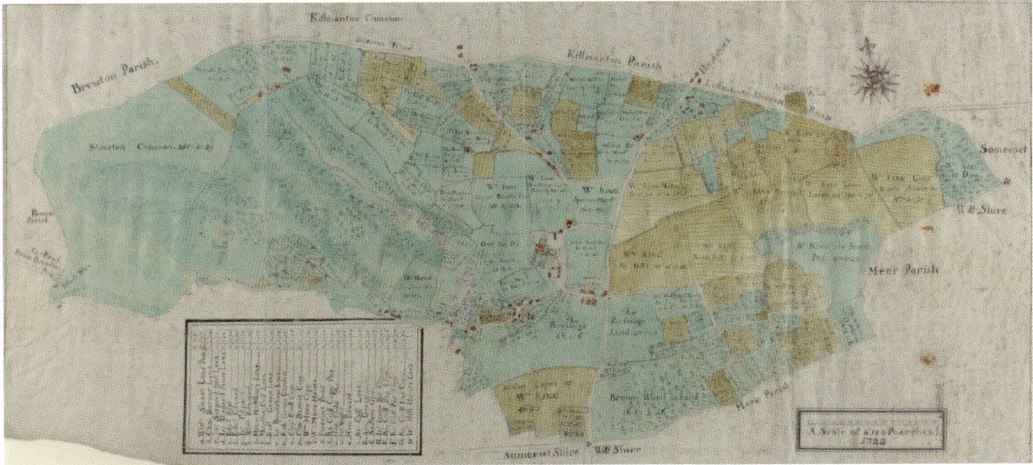

1722 | Estate Map showing river | WHS 383/316 (Map of Stourton 1722)
Image courtesy Wiltshire and Swindon History Centre

Originally a temple dedicated to Diana was placed on the hillside, in her 'grove' among the trees. The lake was known as Speculum Dianae or Diana's Mirror. It is a place of great scenic beauty and has always attracted writers, poets and artists. The view enjoyed special respect among landscape painters, amongst them J.M.W. Turner.

It's easy to see the similarities between Nemi and Stourhead. Although there's no written evidence that Henry visited Lake Nemi, it would seem entirely possible. He later purchased a painting of the idyllic scene, *The Lake of Nemi, with Diana and Callisto*. Why else would he have done this, if not to remind him of a memorable visit? This painting, by Richard Wilson RA, today hangs in the Cabinet Room. Wilson was a Welsh artist who lived in Italy between 1750 and 1757, and who was much sought after at the time. He was the first major British painter to concentrate on landscape painting and was one of the founder members of the Royal Academy. Henry became a patron of one of Wilson's pupils, John Plimmer. In June 1759, Plimmer wrote to Henry and said he was obliged for Henry's advice to take classical views about Naples as Mr Wilson had done and 'As to what you recommend in the management of the leafing of trees, I have endeavoured to imitate Claude and Nature with as much care as I possibly could ever since Mr. Wilson left Rome and I have been my own master'.[6] In July 1760, Plimmer despatched to Henry a copy of a Claude picture in the Galleria Doria-Pamphilj, entitled *Procession to the Temple of Apollo at Delos*. This picture today hangs in the Picture Gallery.

The valley Henry could see far below was his valley, here at Stourhead: the canvas on which Henry would create his own landscape painting.

Henry would have needed help to achieve his vision. He needed an architect to design the temple he planned to build, and a stone mason to execute the work. He commissioned the talented and fashionable architect Henry Flitcroft (1697–1769) to work on the design of the temple.

Three letters survive from the correspondence between Henry and Flitcroft, discussing the finer points of design. They give fascinating clues to Flitcroft's character, his opinions and the relationship between the two men. These letters are dated between August and September 1744, only a year after the death of Susan, yet they are already discussing several plans simultaneously, indicating that Henry must have been giving thought to his ideas soon after her death. The first letter, from Flitcroft and dated 18th August 1744, states: 'I have sent ye Cornice at Large for the Venetian Seat ...'[7] Flitcroft designed this small building; it later became known as the Temple on the Terrace (a detailed description is given in Appendix II).

He then went on to complain about the price the builder, Ireson, proposed to charge but acknowledged that, providing it is done well, it may indeed be costly. He voices his regret that:

> There is too little Art or Care used in most Country Work, but as these
> Examples ought to be well done ... am for having it well done... Not that I would
> give a farthing more than it deserves if not done as I propose.

Surely an eye on finances would appeal to a thrifty banker. Flitcroft continued by discussing the design of a temple he called 'the Circular open Temple of the Dorick Order Antique'. As we know, the Temple of Apollo was not an open temple or of the 'Dorick' order. Perhaps this was an early idea and Henry then changed his mind as to its design. In this letter, Flitcroft also questioned the suitability and quality of the stone: 'you can raise at your Quarry and also must desire to know if it is weather-proof, especially for the crown of the Dome'.

Only a week later, on 25th August 1744,[8] he was again cautioning Henry on the use of his stone for the Round Temple, which he thought would be too small. Again, too, he considered Ireson unreasonable in his demands, suggesting that 'if he is not capable of the work, then some other person should be employed'. He made the point that, if the masonry 'be not excellently well done, it will not answer your purpose in being both a beautiful and lasting piece of work'. Here, Flitcroft was following the advice laid down by Vitruvius, who was much admired by 18th-century architects. Flitcroft emphasised this point by saying that if the execution of the work is not well done:

> ... it will not do justice to this monument. I hope you will transmit to posterity
> to be a credit to the time in which it was done, far too true that Workmen of
> this Age study only their too much profit, rather than to be Expert in Geometry,
> the Mechanicals and the Nature of Materials.

I think Flitcroft would be pleased to know that his attention to detail and insistence on skilled workmanship has most certainly been a credit to his time.

Finally, he promised to send details of the 'Temple of Ceres with the Rocky Arch in which I propose to place the River God'.

The third letter follows in quick succession a week later, on 1st September 1744.[9] Flitcroft enclosed the plan and elevation of the Temple of Ceres, with more detail on the decorative stonework. He also noted that 'if the ground in the place where this building is to stand be Natural Firm Earth, then following the plan and sections will be sufficient to make it a very good building', and 'this will be sufficient to enable you to talk with your Mason about the building'. Flitcroft knew that Henry took a personal interest in the design and construction of the buildings: he was well informed and had enough knowledge to discuss these points with the builder.

Flitcroft went on to design all the buildings in the garden. Between 1744 and 1766, Henry paid him a total of about £1,000.

Twenty-five years after these earlier letters, following the death of Henry Flitcroft, there is a moving and thoughtful letter to Henry from Flitcroft's son, also Henry, dated 4th September 1769. This letter paid tribute to the long working relationship and friendship between the two men. Henry Flitcroft Junior asked that Henry accept a drawing copied by his father from a design by Inigo Jones, 'which I trust his Execution has done justice to his great Original'. He continued by saying:

> I hope you consider it as the best ('tho inadequate) acknowledgement in my power to make of the great obligation I am under to you on my Father's account and my own. This monument to his memory, I commit to your protection, to whose patronage when living, his merit was principally indebted.

William Privett (1726–1763) was the stone mason who took Flitcroft's designs and turned them into solid reality. Henry had employed Privett at Quarley and knew the quality of his work. Maybe he took Flitcroft's advice that if Ireson was not capable of such work, then 'some other person may be employed'. Privett was one of the owners of a large quarry at Chilmark, a village about fifteen miles from Stourhead. He went on to supply the stone and be responsible for the building of all the features in the garden, and there are many payments to him recorded in the ledgers.

Like all good garden designers, Henry made use of what he already had. He positioned the Temple of Ceres at the head of a small rectangular basin which had always been the site of a well supplying water to the village and was known as Paradise Well. The abundant supply of clear, fresh water was provided by a spring emerging onto the surface. Henry must have realised that he could further enhance the temple by turning this simple rectangular pool into an attractive feature – perhaps by extending it and adding Flitcroft's suggestion of a 'Rocky Arch in which I propose to place the River God'. The River God had been purchased by Henry a year earlier, in January 1743, from the sculptor Thomas Manning. This purchase was made four months before the death of Susan, indicating again that Henry may well have been formulating plans even then.

The finished design was captured in a drawing by Bampfylde. It shows the Temple of Ceres, which is quite small, sitting above a straight-sided body of water, at the head of which is a pedimented arch over a rocky recess. The River God is placed inside this recess, reclining on a platform, and the spring gushes out over the platform to create a small cascade. In Bampfylde's picture, the grass on each side of this feature is smooth and there is a figure lying on the grass reading a book. A further figure is fishing in the canal. It has been suggested that this canal was originally made to act as a stew pond for storing live fish until they were needed; catching fish in a confined area was much easier than fishing in a large body of water. This drawing was made in 1753, eight years after the completion of the Temple of Ceres, and well before the lake was in place. It is the first depiction of the garden.

Henry now moved on to enhancing the Fir Walk, which he had created some eleven years earlier, placing an Obelisk at the end as a focal point. The Obelisk was constructed of Chilmark stone by William Privett and his associates, Robert Moor Senior and Robert Moor Junior. Henry must have taken Flitcroft's words of warning to heart: owing to 'some doubt arising to the said Henry Hoare', he demanded that the agreement with these men took the form of a bond or insurance policy against the deterioration of the stone used. Even though Privett had made a good job of the Temple of Ceres, Henry must have thought the Obelisk was a greater risk. He bound Privett and his partners (and not only themselves but 'each and every one of your heirs Executors and Administrators') to a figure of £100 of 'good and lawful money' to be paid in the event of the stone deteriorating. He specified that the stone should endure and 'stand all weather for the Space of five years from the finishing and completing the said Obelisk without receiving any damage thereby either by Shelling flaws or otherwise'. Providing these terms were adhered to, then the 'obligation to be void, otherwise to be and remain in full force'. Henry was a hard, but fair, taskmaster, and he wasn't taking any chances – exactly what you would expect from a prudent banker. The contract for the Obelisk was dated 6th September 1746,[10] signed by all three men and witnessed by Joshua Cox, agent, and Roger Helliker, gardener. Later, a gilded copper disc representing the sun was placed on top of the Obelisk, which sparkles in the morning sun.

Henry now turned his attention to the upper garden close to the house. In his father's day, the large lawn to the south of the house was bounded by stuccoed walls. Original watercolours by J.C. Buckler of this early stage of the garden are shown in Colt Hoare's *Pedigrees and Memoirs of the Families of Hore*.[11] Henry softened the appearance of the garden by removing the wall and planting a double row of beech trees down each side. The existing circular pond containing a statue was removed and he later placed a large statue of Apollo, on a mound, in the same position. Thus, two focal points were created in different directions when looking from the house. The first looks from the saloon on the west side of the house across Great Oar meadow to the Obelisk; the second looks out from the Garden Room on the south side to the statue of Apollo. The Fir Walk joins the two focal points. The statue of Apollo, cast in lead by the sculptor John Cheere, was bought as a pair with a statue of Diana. It is thought he placed the statue of Diana 'in her grove' along the hillside amongst the trees, looking down on one of the smaller ponds. This pond became known as Diana's basin. Lead statues were usually placed outside, as they could withstand the British weather.

These statues were bought in May 1745, just as the Temple of Ceres was nearing completion. It's tempting, therefore, to speculate that Henry's plans were already moving forward. But, of course, he may have bought them simply because he liked them, and only later decided what to do with them. One other thought occurs to me. Apollo and

Diana were twins. Apollo was the God of the Muses – the arts and poetry – and Diana, the Goddess of the Hunt. Did Henry like them because they reflected his twin passions?

Henry may well have taken the idea of the Fir Walk from designs he had already seen. Henry's father had commissioned the garden designer, Stephen Switzer (1682–1745) to draw up plans. The Partners' Ledger shows an early payment to Stephen Switzer: '19th April 1721 Mr Switzer for making plans of my garden'.[12] These plans have never been found, but there are three volumes of Stephen Switzer's published work, *Ichnographia Rustica*, in the Library. Today, Switzer does not attract as much attention as other fashionable garden designers of the time such as William Kent and Charles Bridgeman, but he was certainly competent. This is not surprising: he was trained by two most knowledgeable and successful men – George London and Henry Wise – whose nursery on the Brompton Road in London supplied trees and plants to all the great and good.

This configuration of the Fir Walk was very much in the old style of design, and Sir John Parnell (1744–1801) commented on this when he visited in 1769.[13] Parnell was Chancellor of the Irish Exchequer and made a visit to England to gather ideas for the improvement of his own estate in Ireland. He noted:

> ... you come at once into a noble walk on the very top of the hill, I believe
> 500 yards long, about 40ft. wide or less, terminated at one end with
> a magnificent Obelisk, at the other a fine view open to the country.
> Here, you'll naturally say is a specimen of the old-fashioned straight-lined
> gardens so much decried in the present age. How comes it here in a new
> improvement admired for elegant taste?

He went on to justify to himself this apparent lack of 'taste' in a 'new improvement'. New ideas were referred to as 'improvements' to the landscape. He explained that should this type of 'close sided visto' be the only thing to see in Mr Hoare's garden, then the comment would be valid, but here it is a crowning glory:

> I never mett a better instance of the good effect of introducing a fine walk of
> this kind than here. ... I would always have such a walk as this in every extensive
> improvement ... especially if it is gained on the very summit of the hill, the effect
> will be greater from its being quite unexpected.

So, although the Fir Walk was acknowledged as being 'old school', it did have a place when used sparingly and unexpectedly. Praise indeed.

I was delighted to read that Parnell referred to 'old-fashioned straight-lined' gardens. By the date of Parnell's visit in 1769, the fashion in garden design had changed dramatically. A new style had begun to emerge in England, promoted by Joseph Addison (1672–1719), founder and editor of *The Spectator*. His thoughts took the form of articles in this paper, and he reflected on the strict formality of garden design in this country, copying French and Dutch style. He posed the question: 'Why not abandon these ideas and embrace the beauty of our English countryside?' He went on to ask the owners of large estates: 'Why may not a whole Estate be thrown into a kind of Garden', and '... if the natural Embroidery of the Meadows were helpt and improved by some small Additions of Art ... A Man might make a pretty Landskip of his own Possessions'. He was dismissive of the French taste for topiary – nature forced into a straitjacket – and wrote scathingly:

> Our Trees rise in Cones, Globes and Pyramids. We see the Marks of Scissars upon every Plant and Bush. I do not know whether I am singular in my Opinion, but, for my own part, I would rather look upon a Tree in all its Luxuriancy and Diffusion of Boughs and Branches, than when it is thus cut and trimmed into a Mathematical Figure.[14]

Addison was a journalist, not a gardener. He left it to others to work out how to translate these radical ideas into reality. Nevertheless, this germ of an idea took hold and became a whole movement, eventually becoming known as the English landscape style. Ironically, European landowners and architects then came to England to see what we had been doing, fell in love with this new style and returned to the Continent fired with enthusiasm for re-creating a 'landscape garden' in their own country.

In 1746, then, the garden contained the Fir Walk, terminated by the Obelisk; the statue of Apollo on the south lawn; the Venetian Seat (Temple on the Terrace) and, in the valley, far below, a temple dedicated to Ceres (Temple of Flora).

Henry now needed someone to oversee the further 'improvements' he was planning. Someone whose work he already knew and could trust. Someone whose talent ranked alongside that of Flitcroft and Privett.

In 1747, Francis Faugoin arrived at Stourhead. He was thirty-one.

1 Wiltshire & Swindon History Centre. 1722 Estate Map. 383.316.
2 *The London Chronicle or Universal Evening Post.* No. 73, 16–18 June 1757, p. 578.
3 Cox, O. 'A Mistaken Iconography? Eighteenth-century Visitor Accounts of Stourhead'. *Garden History Society. Journal of Garden History.* 2012. Vol. 40. Issue 1, pp. 98–116.
4 Hoare, Sir Richard Colt, Bt. *A Description of the House, Paintings and Gardens, together with the Museum of Antiquities at Stourhead.* 1818.
5 Dodd, Dudley ed. *The Letters of Henry Hoare 1760–1781.* Wiltshire Record Society, Wiltshire & Swindon History Centre, Chippenham, 2018. p. 85. WSA 1300/3264.
6 Woodbridge, Kenneth. *Landscape and Antiquity, Aspects of English Culture at Stourhead 1718—1838.* Oxford, 1970. p. 46.
7 WSA 383/907.
8 Ibid.
9 Ibid.
10 Ibid.
11 Hoare, Sir Richard Colt, Bt. *Pedigrees and Memoirs of the Families of Hore.* Bath, 1819.
12 C. Hoare & Co. archive: HFM/4/7.
13 Extracts from an unpublished journal by Sir John Parnell, 1769, vol. II, folios 79–113: description of the garden and Perimeter Drive together with notes on the house and art collection, reproduced in an article for the National Trust by Kenneth Woodbridge, 1982. Original manuscript in the British Library.
14 Addison, Joseph. Essay in *The Spectator*, 25 June 1712, cited in Mowl, Timothy. *Gentlemen & Players: Gardeners of the English Landscape.* Sutton Publishing Ltd, 2000. p. 83.

CHAPTER THIRTEEN

THE MAKING
OF THE GARDEN

✦

15 April 1747   Francis Faugoin   £20 os od

I T WAS SUCH a pleasure to see Francis's name appear again in the pages of Henry
Hoare's Ledger of Personal Accounts.

The payments to Francis are recorded in three volumes, covering the years 1734–
1749, 1749–1770, and 1770–1785. They form a continuous record of the money given
to Francis. These ledgers show Henry's personal expenditure: he paid for the creation of
the garden from his own pocket.

Of course, payments to Francis for maintenance of the finished garden continued.
By now he was also acting as Steward, collecting rents and paying in money. Henry
paid Francis the last gratuity of ten guineas on 23rd October 1783. Henry then left
Stourhead and retired to his house in Clapham.

In the absence of accounts kept by Francis, I've used the entries in these ledgers as a
starting point and, through them, have been able to trace Francis's story. These payments
serve to give a chronology which can then be linked to the chronology of the garden.

However, these entries are just the bare bones. I had to find other ways to interpret
the entries in the ledger. I had to keep in mind the monetary sum and relate it to all the
activities carried out at the time. At each stage of the garden's development, I have had
to imagine Francis's contribution represented by these figures and see how his expertise
was brought into play.

As stated previously, it is in 'the Wilberry ledger' that Francis's name appears for
the first time, in July 1736. Then he and Mary marry, and both their names disappear from the ledger. The entry first recording Francis as definitely at Stourhead reads:
'15 April 1747 Francis Faugoin £20'. Why did Francis begin to work at Stourhead at this
precise moment? Because, until that moment, Henry had no need of a head gardener at
Stourhead. The post was already filled.

Roger Helliker had been employed as a gardener by Henry's father, Good Henry, when he began to lay out a garden to surround his newly built house. Helliker was, therefore, the first head gardener at Stourhead. He came from a large family living in nearby Horningsham, on the Longleat estate. His employment continued long after the death of Good Henry in 1725. His name is recorded in 'the Wilberry ledger': 'September 1735 Money paid Roger Helliker at Stourhead £50'.

Good Henry also had the services of Joshua Cox, acting as his agent, whose duties included collecting rents from tenants. The ledger entry reads: 'Money received by Mr. Cox from tenants at Stourton, Stourton Caundle and Knoyle – £150'. Cox continued in this role for Henry's widow, Jane, and later for their son, Henry the Magnificent. Cox was a successful lawyer; both he and Helliker were in positions of trust. Cox rented the house at Quarley for a time, and his son, Richard, later bought the property. Richard went on to fame and fortune when he became a military agent to the Grenadier Guards. Agents arranged payment of officers and men, organised the provision of clothing and requisitioned supplies and weapons. This experience in logistics and welfare of the troops laid the foundation for what was to become the travel agents Cox and Kings.

But in 1747, something clearly changed. From that date, both names, of Helliker and of Joshua Cox, disappear from the ledger. It seems that Francis took over from both these men. Over time, his responsibilities widened from 'the gardener', to acting on behalf of Henry as his agent or steward. There are payments in the ledger indicating that Francis was paying in money received from tenants; he witnessed legal documents relating to the purchase of land and advised interested parties of the particulars of the property at Quarley when it was advertised for 'Lett', being referred to as 'Mr. Francis Faugoin at Stourton'.

We don't know why Helliker ceased to work for Henry. We do know for certain that, in 1747, Henry was focussed on the plans he had in mind for an innovative garden and needed someone with the right skills to help him achieve this ambition. He already had the services of a talented architect and an experienced stone mason, both at the top of their field. He now needed someone equally skilled in horticulture, who could make a significant contribution to the embryo garden but could also manage people. Labourers would need to be hired, materials sourced, problems solved. Henry also needed a person he could trust to be responsible for large amounts of cash, and who he could leave in charge when he was in London working at the bank.

Francis Faugoin was the man for the job.

It's impossible to know at what point Henry understood the full potential of the valley's natural advantages. Perhaps it was at this moment that the idea which had been germinating in his mind for some time began to take shape. Scholars have often debated whether Henry's grand plan sprang fully formed into his head, or evolved, piece by piece, as he went along. Probably, it was a mixture of both. On completion of the Temple of Ceres, it could be argued that what followed – the Wooden Palladian Bridge, the Grotto, the Pantheon, the Lake – were envisaged together. They were, indeed, all under construction simultaneously.

So, the first task for Francis was to oversee the construction of the Temple of the Nymph, today known as the Grotto. The location chosen was on the opposite side of the valley from the Temple of Ceres, slightly above the smallest of the ponds, referred to as the 'withy bed pond'.

The Grotto was not as simple as the Temple of Ceres and included several components. The central chambers were constructed before the planned rise in water level to create the lake. The entrance to the Grotto was partially hidden beneath overhanging trees and laurels, heightening the sense of mystery. Approached through a dark tunnel, uneven cobbles and low light levels slowed the visitor down; the sound of gushing of water could be heard in the distance. This deliberate effect created a frisson of fear and trepidation, which is still felt by visitors today, especially if entering from the bright light of a sunny day. The sudden change from light to dark results in faltering footsteps and a fear of falling. To increase this sense of disorientation and add to the drama, Henry later added an extension to the entrance tunnel. It was with some relief that visitors emerged into a high and domed circular space. On the right, a deep recess held the gleaming white statue of a sleeping nymph, reclining on a block of stone. Water poured round the statue and tumbled down into a sunken pool below. The same design detail had been used by Flitcroft when he placed the statue of the River God in the rocky recess below the Temple of Ceres.

On hot days, Henry bathed in the clear, cold water of this pool. He expressed his delight in a letter to his daughter, Susanna:

> I had a delicious souse into the Cold Bath this morning to The Tunes of
> French Horns playing Round me all the while belonging to Company who lay
> at Our Inn and took the advantage of a second view in the morning.[1]

His widowed niece, Martha (who acted as housekeeper for Henry after the death of his wife and looked after the children), wrote to Henry's younger brother, Richard, that Henry 'has gone into the cold Bath these three mornings (as he says) by way of a treat & comes into breakfast as fresh as a Rose'.

The water from the pool drained under a floor made up of concentric circles of pebbles and emptied into the pond below. Four niches round the walls provided places to sit. Opposite the sunken pool, an arched rocky opening framed a view back across the green valley. Looking out through this opening, towards the church and village in the distance, the two large ponds could still be seen, set in the pasture of the valley floor. Before climbing up the steep steps out of the Grotto, visitors would find another deep recess on the left, which held an impressive statue of a river god with flowing hair and beard. Seated on an urn, which poured forth water, his right hand was raised as if pointing the way out. The climb up and out of this watery abode required effort: the steps are steep and uneven; they change direction; but at last, the visitor gained firmer ground and welcome sunlight.

The Grotto was an ambitious and difficult feature to build. Given its complexity and similarities with the feature in front of the Temple of Ceres, it seems likely to have been designed by Flitcroft and built by Privett, who probably employed workmen from his quarry to assist: Joseph Lane (1717–1784) and his son, Josiah, who went on to build many more grottoes for wealthy patrons.

At the same time as the Grotto was under construction, Francis oversaw the building of a bridge. This was an important early feature in the garden and served a practical purpose after the lake was formed: providing the means of getting from one side of the valley to the other. The bridge was begun in 1749, shortly after the Grotto and before the Pantheon. Henry took the design from Palladio's *The Four Books of Architecture*, Book III, Chapter V, 'Wooden Bridges'.

In 2005, the Nautical Archaeology Society visited Stourhead, surveying the bed of the lake and producing an in-depth report. With their expert knowledge of underwater archaeology, they posed the question: 'Since the Great Lake had not yet been created, were the foundations of the bridge designed and positioned with a view to a subsequent, planned rise in water level?' So, they were suggesting that the bridge was built *before* the water was allowed to flood the valley floor. When this idea is pointed out, it makes perfect sense, but it is still astounding to comprehend the amount of thought and forward planning required.

The bridge is no longer there. Colt Hoare removed it. He records in the Annals:

> In the summer of 1798, I took down the Palladian Bridge, placed a ferry on the same spot.

But it had remained in place for forty-nine years. (A more detailed account of the bridge is given in Appendix I.)

Another early feature in the garden was the Chinese Alcove. It was placed on a hairpin bend on the path winding down to the lake from the Temple on the Terrace. A detailed account of this charming, whimsical little feature is given in Appendix II.

When Francis arrived at Stourhead in 1747, he was thirty-one, Mary thirty, young Henry four and baby Felix one year old. One year later, Francis and Mary celebrated the birth of their third son, John, baptised on 2nd December 1748 in Stourton church. By this date, the two older boys were five and two years old, and Henry's children were growing up: Henry Junior eighteen, Susanna sixteen and Anne eleven. It's easy to imagine the younger ones being excited by all this activity. Henry later recorded his grandchildren's pleasure in the Grotto – 'the Temple of the Nymph is all enchantment to them' – but there is no record of his own children's reaction.

Two years later, Henry Junior was now old enough to embark on his own Grand Tour. With his companion, John Rust, he set off for the Continent. Rust was eight years older than Henry Junior and the brother of Elizabeth Rust, the second wife of Henry the Magnificent's younger brother, Sir Richard Hoare. On Christmas Day 1750, Henry Junior wrote a long letter to his father from Aix-en-Provence,[2] where Henry and Susan had stayed for over a year during their own Grand Tour. Presumably, Henry recommended staying in Aix on their way south, and it seems that Henry had tasked him with visiting galleries on the way and reporting back to him on the art he saw. This letter reveals Henry Junior's extensive knowledge: he could evaluate the merits, or otherwise, of what he was seeing. Obviously, he had been well schooled by his father and proved to be an attentive pupil.

The letter began with a flimsy apology familiar to all parents: an excuse for not writing sooner. 'I intended to have wrote yesterday to you, but being interrupted, I put it off till today and not finding myself in good spirits on account of a slight head-ache, I have desir'd my Friend to be my secretary.' No doubt his 'headache' stemmed from rather too much Christmas cheer the previous evening. I don't think he fooled his father, who could remember only too well his own youthful excesses. Henry Junior made up for this apology by giving detailed descriptions of many paintings. He continues by describing a Claude, commenting:

> It is remarkable for having a Jupiter & Europa in the foreground; it is a seaport with Trees on the left hand, & on the Right a Castle on the Top of a Rock projecting into the sea, which you see through some Trees. It is a pleasant picture but not a warm one & neither that nor any of the others are in good preservation enough for you to buy.

He then described the paintings he saw in 'the Luxembourg'. In 1750, the Luxembourg Palace in Paris became a museum and art gallery, the forerunner of the Louvre, which was not opened until 1793. 'As to the Pictures in the Luxembourg, I shall give you an account of some of the best. They are marked in my Catalogue ...'

He proceeded to give descriptions of an astonishing number of paintings:

> The first is an Andrea del Sarto representing Charity & her three children. The Design of it is extravagant & bigger than Life: remarkable for having been taken off from board & put upon Canvas ... two pictures of N. Poussin, the Plague among the Philistines and the Manna, they are two of his finest Works. Another of the same Master, the Rape of the Sabines, very indifferent ... A small Rembrandt, the Angel flying away from Tobit who is kneeling, it has a great effect. St. Bruno in the Desart by Mola, a very fine Picture. The Roman Charity by Guido, Dark & done in the manner of Caravaggio. There are two whole rooms of French Painters ... St. Michael Treading on the Devil, a small picture [by Raphael (*inserted in margin*)], it is [en]grav'd in Crozat's Collection. The figure of St. Michael fine & the Devils very strange. An holy family of Titian, the Virgin holding a white Rabbit in her hand, exquisitely Colour'd. St. George & the Dragon by Raphael, a Companion to the St. Michael.

This is just a small selection of the many paintings he describes, finishing the letter:

> These are the Pictures most worth mentioning & in my next Letter I will finish the account of the Palais Royal.
>
> I hope soon to hear of your continuing in good health & am,
> With Complts to all, Honour'd Sir, your Most Dutifull Son, | HENRY HOARE.

As the Palais Royal was another art gallery in Paris, it would seem that Henry Junior and John Rust stayed there for a short time en route to Aix, where they spent Christmas, before journeying south to Italy. We have no record of the sights and treasures Henry Junior encountered there until he arrived in Naples just over a year later.

Then disaster struck.

The *Salisbury Journal* recorded an entry from *The London Gazette*.

> The *Salisbury Journal* March 1752 News from the London Gazette
> Letters from Naples advise, that on the 5th February died there, of the
> Small Pox, Henry Hoare, jun. Esq. only Son of Henry Hoare Esq., Sir Richard's
> Elder Brother. He had been near two Years on his Travels, improving a Mind
> endowed with every good and amiable Quality, and a Genius remarkably
> adapted to most Parts of Polite and useful Science.

What a bitter, bitter blow for his father: his only remaining son and heir dying of disease, far away from home. He must have been so proud of Henry, looking forward to guiding him in business and banking in preparation for the time when he would become a partner in the family firm. He would have enjoyed passing on his knowledge of art and would have been eagerly awaiting his son's return from Italy. All his hopes and dreams and plans for the future were swept away in one devastating blow.

Smallpox was probably the single most lethal cause of death in the 18th century. A high fever, severe headache and vomiting was followed by a widespread rash, which developed into fluid-filled blisters. Those lucky enough to survive were left with disfiguring scars and often blindness.

This dreadful news caused consternation when it was first received. There was a flurry of letters back and forth between friends and family. Not wishing to alarm Henry unnecessarily, Henry Junior's companion in Naples, John Rust, wrote firstly to his brother-in-law, James Whitchurch, who was a member of the extended family. He told him that Henry had contracted the 'Small Pox' but, having a 'good English Physician' and the best nursing available in Naples, he 'had great hopes he would get over it', and went on to say '... thought it not proper to acquaint his Father, as he knew how little able he would be to bear the dreadfull Suspense'.[3]

Sadly, another letter from John Rust confirmed that Henry Junior did not recover but died on 16th February 1752. By now, Sir Richard, Henry's brother, and Charles Wray, Chief Clerk at the bank, were aware of the situation. Before telling Henry, they asked Whitchurch to pass this news to Joshua Cox. Wishing to shield Henry from too great a shock, they asked that Cox broke the news in person, before a letter arrived from Rust confirming the death:

> ... In the mean time Sir you will take the Most favourable opportunity
> of breaking it to him & in such a Manner as may least shock his tender Nature.
> And you will please to add that no Assistance was wanting, my Bro'r Rust
> attending him constantly, tho' he never had the distemper himself ...[4]

Sir Richard then asked Cox to take care of the arrangements for mourning. He assured him that, for his part, he would now take care of the 'Gentlemen in the Shop' (employees at the bank) and asked that he be remembered to all other friends. He also said:

> ... I took the Earliest Opportunity, My Depressed Spirits, & Afflicted Heart
> would Permit me to Write to him, & if any Expression should Drop from him,
> that my Coming down would be Agreeable, I beg you would lett me know ...
> The Satisfaction of Seeing his own hand Writeing was a Comfort to me ....[5]

Upon hearing this devastating news, Henry wrote to Joshua Cox, asking him to be guided by Sir Richard when it came to making arrangements for the mourning period. He also asked Cox to write to Mr Rust, explaining that he felt unable to write directly himself at this time, but that if Rust found it too difficult to return to England immediately, he would pay any expenses incurred and 'when He returns My hope depends on passing the remains of my Life with Him'.[6]

Henry wrote a moving letter to his brother on 14th March 1752:

> My Dearest Brother
> Yours and my Dear Sisters most Tender concern for me under my severe
> affliction melts down my Soul with Love and Affection towards you ...

That deeply emotional phrase 'melts down my soul', illustrates the close and loving bond Henry had with his brother and sisters, and his willingness to share with them his grief and despair.

In another letter to his brother two years later, not surprisingly, Henry still refers to his loss and the emotional scars he bears:

> *8th September 1754*
> My Dear Brother ... it was at that time the only resource of comfort to my
> wounded Spirit. on The Loss of that Person whose memory will ever be most
> Dear to me, & for whom my Heart in its last beating moment will bleed afresh:
> but alas! I cannot bring Him back again.[7]

Once again, Henry had no option but to get on with life. His presence as Senior Partner of the bank was essential, and the continuation of his plans for Stourhead must have provided a welcome distraction. So, it was full steam ahead, or as Henry remarked, '*con spirito*'. He now had to turn his full attention to the design and building of a truly ambitious feature: the Temple of Hercules, otherwise known as the Pantheon.

The paintings bought by Henry provide clues as to influences and inspirations. Henry was always keen to acquire works of art from the great masters he so admired. Not long after returning from Italy, he'd attended a sale of the entire contents of Cannons, the house belonging to James Brydges, first Duke of Chandos. The house was the focus of the duke's artistic patronage. Brydges filled Cannons with old masters and Grand Tour acquisitions. Such was the fame of Cannons that great numbers of the public flocked to visit the estate in Little Stanmore, Middlesex.

Brydges died in 1744, and his debts were by then so great that his heirs had no choice but to sell the house and contents in an auction on 16th June 1747. It was at this sale that Henry bought the painting by Nicolas Poussin called *The Choice of Hercules*.

The painting shows the hero, Hercules, standing at the base of a steep, rock-strewn hillside. On his right, a female figure, clad in simple white clothes, is indicating the difficult ascent to the top, but on his left a more seductive figure wearing gold, with flowers in her hair, is suggesting an easier route.

Henry must have been delighted to acquire a genuine Poussin. But did the subject matter of this picture perhaps resonate with him? Hercules was renowned for his ingenuity and strength in the face of adversity. Perhaps the hero was a role model for Henry. Did he see himself as having the mental strength, rather than physical strength, to overcome the difficulties he had faced in the past and would face in the future? The Temple of Ceres and the Grotto were completed, but Henry had more ambitious ideas yet. Would he have the determination to carry on and complete everything he planned, or would it be easier to give up now? Henry had a choice: take the difficult route or choose an easier life.

We know from his character that giving up was not an option.

Henry may have remembered the Temple of Hercules in Rome. The design, however, he modelled on the Pantheon. It's not an exact copy but an inspired interpretation by Flitcroft. Only two weeks after purchasing *The Choice of Hercules*, Henry signed a contract with Rysbrack for a larger-than-life-sized statue of Hercules, who is shown leaning on his club with the skin of the Nemean lion. Henry commissioned this statue after seeing a terracotta model in Rysbrack's yard. Rysbrack left this small model in his will as a gift to Henry for his patronage and friendship. Today, it stands on the desk in the Library.

The contract was signed on 1st July 1747, witnessed by John Wootton. It stated 'in Consideration of the sum of three Hundred pounds, the said Michael Rysbrack shall make a Hercules in Statuary marble ... and shall be finish'd according to the model agreed on within the space of two years and Half ...'. The final payment was made on 9th July 1752, and on 16th July 1757 Henry paid an extra £50 in the form of a gratuity as he was so pleased with the result – the crowning glory for his new temple. The statue is signed and dated 1756 but was not installed until the completion of the interior of the building in 1761. Henry later wrote in a letter to his daughter, Susanna, 'I thought old Rysbrack would have wept for Joy to see His offspring placed to such advantage. He thinks it impossible for such a space to have more magnificence in it and striking awe than He found there.'[8]

I've never forgotten the first time I saw the Pantheon in Rome, when Anne and I did our own 'grand tour'. The first thought that sprang into my mind was: 'What ambition, what daring, to decide to build a copy of this – in your own garden'. Today, the Pantheon at Stourhead remains the focal point of the garden and the view of it across the lake is the one that many people recognise. In its way, it is just as iconic as the real thing.

The Choice of Hercules
NICOLAS POUSSIN (1594–1665)
Oil painting on canvas | circa 1636–37 | © National Trust Images/Prudence Cuming

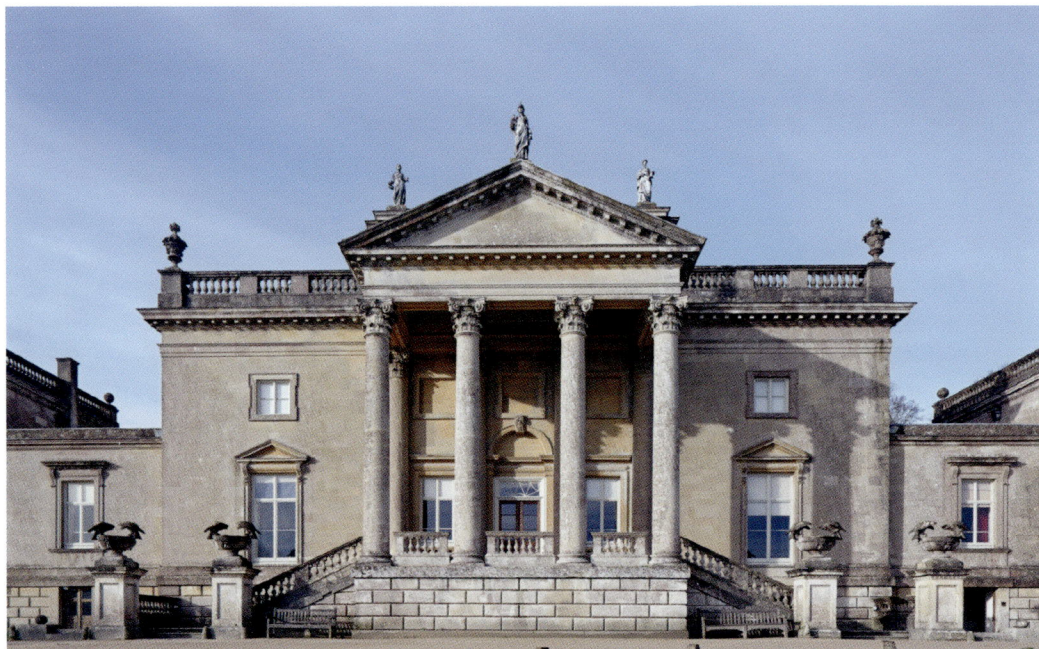

The exterior of the house at Stourhead, Wiltshire | © National Trust Images/Dennis Gilbert

Information about this early stage of the garden also comes from visitor accounts. The first known visitor to Stourhead to record what he saw there was Dr Richard Pococke (1704–1765), an Irish Bishop, born in Southampton, best known for travel writings and diaries.[9] He had visited France and Italy and travelled extensively in the Far East. He spent his later years touring Ireland and Britain, publishing accounts of his journeys.

On 2nd July 1754, he spent time looking round Stourhead house, beginning his tour of the garden from the south lawn.

> The South of the house is a lawn with a piece of water and from that is a winding descent over the above-mentioned valley ... and below, over the water, is an Ionick temple. Below this are two large pieces of water, which are to be made into one and much enlarged, for which a head is making at great expence. There are to be three islands in it with different kinds of buildings in them, one of which is to be a Mosque with a Minaret.

How exciting to have a Mosque on one of the islands. Henry clearly changed his mind on that idea. Pococke continues:

> ... On the other side of the water is a very beautiful grotto, with cascades of water at the end falling down in streams about the river God. ...but the most magnificent building is the Temple of Hercules, not yet finished ... the prospect from this spot is very beautiful ...

Here we have clear confirmation that the two existing ponds are going to be 'made into one and much enlarged', that the dam (head) is being planned and the Pantheon is not yet finished. All in all, a large amount of planning, construction and labour was needed to carry out the work. It was a colossal undertaking and needed the careful and methodical management, forward planning and organisation of labour that Francis had the ability to carry out.

A hitherto unknown early visitor was Dr Thomas Evans, the Archdeacon of Worcester Cathedral. He recorded his visits to cathedrals and great houses in a travel diary. This came to light only recently, when Anne was researching Head Gardeners of Dorset. His name came up and Anne discovered that this diary was held in the Rare Book and Manuscript Library of Duke University in Durham, North Carolina, USA. She emailed the library and was delighted to learn that the diary had been digitised. On receiving the digital copy, she was even more delighted to see a totally unexpected account of a visit to Stourhead made by Dr Evans in August 1755. These serendipitous discoveries are what makes research so fascinating: when looking for one thing, another pops up.

The diary[10] begins with 'An excursion from Salisbury (80 miles) to Longleate (Lord Weymouth's) with description' and moves on to 'Mr. Hoare's at Stourton'. Dr Evans begins the account in the house:

> ... It is now a most completely elegant House fitted up in the highest taste
> & furnished with an admirable collection of pictures. In the Hall there is a
> good one of Mr. Hoare on Horseback. The Horse is done by Wotton and the
> Figure by Dahl.

> The Salon is 45ft. by 30ft. which seems to be a more pleasing proportion than
> the double cube of 60ft. by 30ft. at Wilton. It contains the following Pictures
> (beginning on the left hand side of the Door.)

> 1. The Daughter of Herodias with the Head of John the Baptist.
> 2. The Rape of Helen – both copies from Guido.
> 3. K. Charles I's three children copied from Vandyke.
> 4. The Death of Dido a fine copy.
> 5. Venus & the Graces.
> 6. Judgment of Midas. An original and capital picture.
> 7. Andromeda chain'd to a Rock.
> 8. Hercules & Wisdom.

Evans gives a detailed account of the Pope's Cabinet and then moves on to the garden:

> The side of the hill on which the House stands is laid out in Walks with Temples
> in the bottom, the River Stour winds itself along and affords a constant supply
> to a large piece of Water which with an island or two in the middle of it looks
> extremely beautiful. A Chinese Bridge over this River leads to a Bath House
> built with huge rough stones. It is call'd the Grotto of the Nymphs ...

He gives an interesting description of the Pantheon:

> There is a walk leading from the Grot to the Temple of Hercules which is a Rotunda, unfinish'd and is to receive in the centre a fine statue of Hercules which Mr. Rysbrack has employ'd ... skill into finishing. The Building will cost £3,000, exclusive of Hercules & Inside ornaments being built upon Arches on account of its nearness to the Water. The Dome alone cost £500 and the Capitals of the Pillars of the Portico which are only Portland Stone cost £25.

He also mentions Terrace Ride.

> A Terrace Walk is now making which is to be 5 miles long and 200 ft. wide. Three thousand pounds a year have been laid out upon these Gardens for ten years last past: the same sum must be expended upon them for several years to come before the vast Improvements that are intended can be executed.

Here is confirmation that Henry was planning further improvements as early as August 1755, when the lake had only just been formed and the Pantheon not yet finished. It can only be assumed that Dr Evans was given these figures by Henry when conducting his visitor round the garden.

That same year, 1755, the traveller and philanthropist Jonas Hanway (1712–1786) stayed at Stourhead as a guest of Henry. He had travelled through Russia and Persia in his younger years, and on returning to live in London, founded the Marine Society to train young men to become seamen. He went on to become Governor of the Foundling Hospital. His account of this visit was published in 1756[11] and was reproduced later anonymously in *The London Chronicle* in June 1757.

He described the house in some detail but paid more attention to the garden, saying:

> I am never half an Hour in a fine House in the Country, without Impatience to walk into the open Air. On the brow of this Hill is a Walk of considerable Extent, of the finest mossy Turf, bordered on each side by stately Scotch Firs of Mr. Hoare's own planting, about 24 Years since. ... This noble broad Walk is terminated by an Obelisk one hundred and twenty Feet in Height ... This Obelisk is divided from the Garden by an Ha-ha, but the View of the Sheep feeding at the Foot of it, has as delightful an Effect as if there was no such Separation.

Hanway confirms the presence of a ha-ha separating the west front of the house from the pasture beyond. He then goes on to describe the 'several irregular walks' leading into the valley. These are 'covered by stately Trees and receive the most heightened Charms by a large Piece of Water at the Bottom on which there is a very pretty Boat'. No doubt he noted more 'heightened charms' when observing 'the female rower, whose Vivacity induced her to try her Skill ... We made a coasting Voyage on the little enchanting Ocean where we discovered several little Islands.' Hanway's report of 1755 has now confirmed the existence of a 'large Piece of Water', and described it as 'the little enchanting Ocean'.

There follow detailed accounts of the Temple of the Nymph, the Temple of Hercules and the Temple of Ceres. Hanway indicated future plans, saying: 'Mr. Hoare has formed his Plan for extending his Walks upon the Brow of the Hill, through his Park for near five miles.' This extended walk became known as Terrace Ride. Hanway then concluded: 'Here we ought to contemplate not only what delights, but what does not shock. In this delicious Abode are no Chinese Works' so Hanway, correctly, does not identify the Palladian arched bridge as 'Chinese'. He continues '... no Monsters of the Imagination, no Deviations from Nature, under the fond Notions of Fashion or Taste: all is grand or simple, or a beautiful Mixture of both'. Even at this early date, when the garden was unfinished, it had begun to cast its spell over visitors.

So, between July 1754 and August 1755, these visitor accounts confirm the completion of the lake, the creation of which was surely the most difficult part of Henry's grand scheme. As Pococke noted, 'Two large pieces of water which are to be made into one'. Henry must have realised use could be made of the existing medieval dam.

In 2005, the Nautical Archaeology Society concluded that:

> A very significant part of the structure must have been present as early as 1722. Henry simply added another 1.5 metres to its height, extended it sideways across the river valley and possibly reinforced and thickened it and controlled its drainage in order to flood the valley.

So, Henry made use of the existing medieval dam by extending it and adding to the height.

A stone retaining wall delineating the serpentine shape of the lake would also have been needed, to prevent soil and vegetation slipping into the lake. That wall would obviously have had to be constructed before the valley was flooded. It followed the contours of the land and is still there, submerged below the water; when the water level is lowered, it can be seen. In view of all this construction work, and controlling and managing a river, I don't think the creation of the lake was 'simple' at all.

The experience and skills gained by Francis when working at Ditton House were now to stand him in good stead and must have been brought into play as he helped Henry to make the great lake a reality. He would have recalled that Duke John had created several water features and made use of a river to create a lake with an island. He had seen this done before.

However, life didn't always proceed smoothly. Jean and I visited the bank to see a small collection of letters to various members of the family.[12] One of these letters described a dramatic event. Henry is writing from Stourhead to his nephew, Richard. The letter is undated, but an approximate date can be calculated, as in it he refers to waiting for news of the 'shocking account fully and truly related of the Earth Quake at Lisbon'. On 1st November 1755, a huge earthquake devastated most of Lisbon. I quote the rest of the letter in full.

Monday was 3 weeks my Large Water was convulsed now upon a Sudden that side next the Pantheon overflowd the Head in an Instant and the other side next where the Waste Water goes off overflowd prodigiously and run down over the Head a Vast Torrent and Labourers and Francis who saw it ran to it with spades thinking the New Head was bursting out. When they came up it was stopt. Francis then let off 2 feet of Water ... not knowing what could be the cause and that caused a Report in Dorset that the Head was down – all friends were at Quarley or Sarum.

What a shock! And what an exciting snippet of information! It must have been an alarming moment for Francis to see a 'vast torrent' flowing over the newly built dam; but, thanks to his quick thinking, he was able to plug the gap with the help of several labourers. This letter also gives us the information that a mechanism was in place to 'let off 2 feet of Water'. It's also revealing that Henry referred to Francis by his first name, indicating an easy familiarity at a time when the role of master and servant was clearly defined.

These early years of making the garden were crowded with activity. It must have looked like a building site. By 1755, the dam was in place and, by careful management of the flow of the river, the water was allowed to flood the valley floor. The outflow, or 'waste water', as Henry called it in his letter, was carried away in a large diameter pipe under the road, emptying back into the river below the dam. It had taken ten years from the completion of the Temple of Flora in 1745 to the flooding of the valley floor to create the Lake in 1755. This was an enormous undertaking, requiring vision, thought, practical skills, problem solving and a certain amount of daring.

1 Dodd, Dudley, ed. *The Letters of Henry Hoare 1760–1781*. Wiltshire Record Society, Wiltshire & Swindon History Centre, Chippenham, 2018. p. 82. WSA 9/35/165(1)/117.

2 WSA 383/907.

3 C. Hoare & Co. archive: HFM/9/8/5.

4 Ibid.

5 C. Hoare & Co. archive: HFM/9/8/6.

6 Ibid. HFM/9/10/1.

7 Ibid. HFM/9/10/4.

8 Dodd, Dudley, ed. *The Letters of Henry Hoare 1760–1781*. Wiltshire Record Society, 2018, p. 43. WSA 1300/4280.

9 Cartwright, J.J., ed. *The Travels through England of Dr. Richard Pococke*, Vol. II, p. 43.

10 Evans, Thomas. *Diary of Travel in England and Wales, 1755–1759*. pp. 27–32. David M. Rubenstein Rare Book & Manuscript Library, Duke University, Durham, North Carolina, USA.

11 Hanway, Jonas. *A Journal of Eight Days Journey from Portsmouth to Kingston upon Thames ... in a Series of Sixty Four Letters Addressed to Two Ladies of the Partie ... by a Gentleman of the Partie*. London, 1756. p. 87.

12 Letters by Henry Hoare to members of his family 1752–1755 (14 items). C. Hoare & Co archive: HFM/9/10.

CHAPTER FOURTEEN

PINEAPPLES, PEOPLE AND PLANTS

⁂

I'VE BEEN ABLE to track down the life of Francis with the help of so many people, but an important element of this story has remained elusive.

What did he actually do?

He was clearly involved in managing the day-to-day activities required to create the garden but, as he was referred to as a 'gardener', his skills were presumably also needed in this capacity. All the payments to Francis are listed in Henry's ledgers of personal accounts from 1736 to 1783, but none of them give any details. Only the payment of ten guineas as a gratuity is specific. The early payments from July 1736 to December 1738 referred to work carried out at Quarley. Then payments ceased until 1747, when Francis arrived at Stourhead. Henry made payments from April to December that year, corresponding to work done on the Grotto and the Obelisk. From then on, payments can be related to each phase of creating the garden and are shown several times a month for each year. This money would have been needed to pay for labour and materials. Henry himself paid the architect, artists and senior craftsmen separately.

But also embedded in these payments would be wages for Francis, and wages for his team of gardeners – who were in addition to the labourers. The 'materials' in this case were for trees and 'greens' in general, equipment, and hands-on, everyday gardening activities, including growing fruit in the walled garden and vegetables in the kitchen garden. Tantalisingly, it's impossible to separate these payments; that separation would have been done in the accounts kept by Francis, which are missing. We can be sure, however, that an eagle-eyed banker would not have employed someone who could not keep accurate accounts.

Dudley found two letters from Francis to Lord Bruce when he was examining the Ailesbury archive, held at the Wiltshire & Swindon History Centre. Thomas Brudenell-Bruce, later first Earl of Ailesbury, was Henry's son-in-law (Susanna's second husband) and he lived at Tottenham Park with his family. The first letter is dated 1766,[1] the second 1771.[2] These letters give us a detailed account of the practical, day-to-day activities of Francis and his team.

Francis is writing to Mr Mackeleath, Lord Bruce's Steward. He begins by asking him to 'present our Dutys to Lord and Lady Bruce' with 'many thanks for the Venison'. It came as a surprise that Francis was receiving a gift of venison. It was a much prized and special meat and was only available if you were rich enough to own a herd of deer and extensive land on which they could roam. The main purpose of the letter is to discuss the availability and price of grass seed. Francis has made enquiries about the Marle Grass Seed and found the seed to be good this year, but more expensive. He has ordered two hundred pounds of 'the Purple sort which has a Greener look in Grass then the White sort'.

He finishes the letter by saying, 'My wife joyns me in compliments to you and Mrs. Bossill – her mother and relations are all well.' It is clear from this letter that Francis knows his counterpart at Tottenham Park well; not only that, but Mary, his wife, is also on friendly terms.

FRANCIS'S LETTER TO LORD BRUCE, 16 MARCH 1771 (THE PINEAPPLE HOUSE LETTER)

Here, Francis is replying directly to a letter from Lord Bruce. It is a wonderful letter, confirming the presence of a pineapple house at Stourhead, with exact descriptions and measurements. Francis explains that the Stourhead pineapple house has been built to a plan 'Mr. Richard Hoare had from me', when he also wished to build one at Barn Elms and, therefore, 'I can let your Lordship have it.' Mr. Richard Hoare was Henry's younger brother. This plan must have been readily available, but it's clear that Francis had the knowledge and confidence to alter the plan for the better and improve on the design.

> We did not exactly follow the Plan as that is, as I remember, all in one house, only parted with Glass between each house. Ours here are three separate houses which we thought to be the Best, for if the insects get into one house they may be Destroyed and not infect the whole.

Francis refers to the fact that Stourhead had three separate glass houses. The Nursery House was used for propagation from crowns: these were small young plants. The next was the Succession House, where one-year-old plants, requiring more space and light, were grown on. Finally, the main house was for fruiting pines. At Stourhead, Francis wisely recommended that these should be three separate houses, to avoid any infestation by insects.

Another alteration was to place brackets on the back wall to support the roof, 'leaving it all clear in the house and not any obstructions as in the Drawing'. This would have allowed more light into the pineapple house. The front supports for the roof 'rest on the side of the Tan Pitt'. I quote the rest of the letter in full: it gives a detailed description of the whole arrangement and a sense of the scale:

> In the Middle the Fruiting house is 40 foot Long and 18 foot Wide,
> the Back Wall 14 foot high from the footpath and the front six foot high.
> The measure is taken from the Outside to the Outside. The Nursery house laid
> 30 foot long and 18 foot Wide from Outside to Outside, the Back Wall 13 foot
> high and the front 5ft high which is enough for the Nursery House.

Francis also mentions the 'Tan Pitt', which was a brick-built space containing tanners' bark. Tanners' bark was a by-product of the leather industry. Crushed oak bark was soaked in water to extract the tannin used to convert animal hides into leather. When the liquid became weaker and ceased to produce tannin, the now-fermenting bark was thrown out as waste and used by gardeners to heat greenhouses and hotbeds. There were three grades of tanners' bark: coarse, medium and fine – and medium was the best. Tanners' bark was judged to be better than manure for heating houses because it gave a more even and long-lasting heat. The bark was placed on a bed of rubble where it maintained a suitable temperature for three to six months. The pines grew in pots sunk into the bark.

I consulted a friend and fellow volunteer, Michael Plaskitt, about these measurements and he was taken aback by the size. This pineapple house was huge. We subsequently paced out the measurements in the walled kitchen garden. The garden is built on a southeast-facing slope, divided into three levels. Only the top level is big enough to take such a structure; it has a high wall at the back. The glass houses would have been built in front of this wall and supported by it.

In his letter, Francis continues by saying that he would be happy to provide further instructions if needed and suggests that it would be a good idea if Lord Bruce's work-men could see these houses 'as the Journey will not be much'. He also offers the services of the bricklayer who built the Stourhead houses: 'he will not have much business this Summer as we do not go on with the building Alfred's Tower, and, therefore, could wait on your Lordship'. As further proof of the cordial relationship between the Faugoins and the rest of Lord Bruce's family, he concludes by saying:

> We are sorry to hear Lady Bruce is so indifferent in health and heartily hope she will get better as the Clapham air agrees with her Ladyship. Mrs. Faugoin rejoyces with me that Master Bruce and Miss Boyle is so well recovered from the Measles.
>
> Mrs. Faugoin joyns me in most respectful Duty to your Lordship, Lady Bruce, Master Bruce, Miss Boyle and young Ladies and am my Lord,
> Your Lordships Dutyfull Servant, | FRANCIS FAUGOIN.

Master Bruce is Susanna and Lord Bruce's first-born son, George. The 'young ladies' are their daughters, Caroline and Frances. Miss Boyle is Henrietta (Harriot), the daughter of Susanna's first husband, Viscount Dungarvan, and she lived with the rest of the family at Tottenham Park.

It is entirely due to Dudley's diligence that we have such revealing insights into Francis's world.

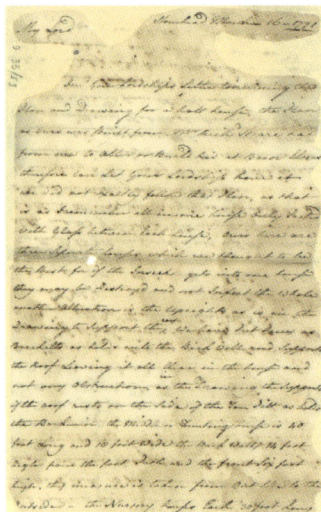

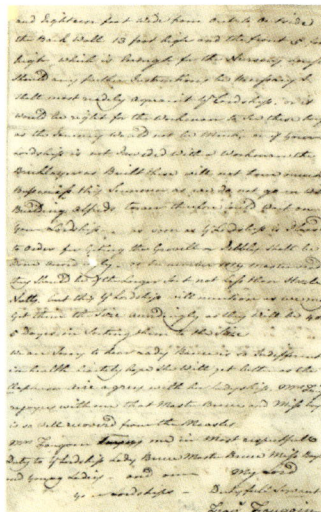

Six years earlier, on 9th December 1765, Henry wrote to Lord Bruce, 'The Pine Apple your Lordship was so good to bestow on us was the largest fruit I ever saw at this season. We know not which to commend most, your Lordship's venison, or Pines which make our mouths water.'[3] People thought the fruit looked similar to a pine cone, but tasted sweet like an apple: hence, 'Pine Apple'. The taste was described as if 'Wine, Rosewater and Sugar were mixed together'.

Pineapples were the ultimate luxury food. They became symbols of status and hospitality and were proudly displayed on all the best dinner tables. Carved stone replicas placed at the entrance to your house proclaimed a warm welcome and a delicious dinner for your guests. If the establishment was not wealthy enough, or large enough, to own extensive glass houses and have the benefit of a talented head gardener, the aspiring hostess could always resort to renting a pineapple for the evening – one guinea each, or two if eaten!

Traders of the Dutch West India Company brought pineapples to Europe from the Caribbean in the early 1600s, giving the Dutch an early advantage in pioneering cultivation methods. This was a challenging task: propagating and growing tropical fruit in the cold, grey climate of Europe. The first person to successfully produce a fruit in Europe was a Dutch woman, Agnes Block, in 1687.[4] The first reliable record of a crop being grown in England was in 1721, by Henry Telende (a Dutchman), gardener to Sir Matthew Decker at his home in Richmond, Surrey.[5] From this date onwards, successfully growing pineapples became an obsession with the aristocracy and landed gentry in Georgian society.

I should perhaps mention the famous, and controversial, painting of John Rose, gardener to Charles II, presenting a pineapple to the King. A copy of this painting hangs in Ham House. The Dutch artist Hendrick Danckerts painted this scene in 1675, showing Rose on bended knee presenting the pineapple on a terrace, with a formal garden and imposing mansion in the background. This painting has always been a mystery and almost all the details have been disputed by experts: date, place, artist, even the identity of the kneeling figure. Doubt stems from the fact that there is no known evidence that pineapples could be successfully grown in England until well after the death of both Rose (1677) and the King (1685). An article by John Royle in the *Journal of Garden History* (1995) gives much detail on the subject.[6] Details of the painting's provenance can also be found at the Lewis Walpole Library in Yale, Connecticut.[7]

The cultivation of home-grown pineapples in the middle of the 18th century was a skilled job, requiring from the owner deep pockets and the services of a knowledgeable head gardener. As pineapples were tropical fruits which grew all year round in their native South America, they demanded careful management to achieve the same year-round production.

An abundance of fruit was grown in the walled garden at Stourhead, which was designed primarily for this purpose. In spring, the attractive blossom of apples and pears was much admired. On the warm brick walls, plums, peaches and apricots were trained into decorative patterns. Hotbeds provided melons, and a vinery produced luscious dessert grapes. Henry referred to strawberries when he imagined little Harriot crushing them into her mouth, followed by 'Ice Cream at the Heals of Them'. Gardeners were expected to produce many different varieties of fruit in the peak of perfection; Henry referred to twenty different sorts of strawberries. The *pièce de résistance*, of course, was the large pineapple house, designed by Francis. The gardener's skill reflected well on their employers, who enjoyed basking in praise from their guests.

One such guest was the diarist James Woodforde, who lived nearby in Castle Cary. On 6th August 1768, he accompanied his friend Justice Creed on a visit to the Hoares, where he was introduced to Henry and members of his family. His diary recorded the event and he commented, 'We had a very elegant dinner and noble Desert of Fruit after – Pine Apple, Melon &c Claret, Madeira &c to drink'.[8]

On 30th November 1771, Henry sent an amusing letter to his adored granddaughter, Harriot:

> I shall on Tuesday next send over to Tottenham Park 35 strong good Fruiting
> pine plants and each will have a Pot in case they should be sick in their Journey
> and I shall gladly accept some West India plants when Our Dearest Lord
> abounds in Them, and till They come, I can supply Him with more and mine
> are said to be a very good sort and many pine after Them.[9]

No doubt Parson Woodforde was one of those who 'pined' after one and probably enjoyed regaling his own guests with accounts of this memorable dinner. It is astonishing to realise that Henry had so many fruiting pines, he was able to spare thirty-five for Lord Bruce – and this at the end of November.

Francis's two letters from the Ailesbury archive are very precious. They give a direct and rare account of what was happening in the garden at the time. They also give a personal insight into Francis's relationship with members of the family.

S ADLY, HENRY NEVER kept a diary of his plans for the garden, or the work carried out. We must rely on comments from visitors, newspaper articles and some of the people he employed as a means of piecing together the overall picture. This lack of a record is the reason Richard Colt Hoare was motivated to begin writing the Annals. His instruction at the beginning is clear.

> From the regret I feel in not knowing at what period many of the buildings were erected, and many of the trees planted, at Stourhead, I have determined that my successors shall not feel the same. I have, therefore, regularly from the year 1792 entered in this book the principal occurrences which regard the Stourhead demesne and I recommend to my successors at that place, the following maxim – do thou, likewise.

Francis needed a large team of gardeners to maintain such a diverse garden. Any gardener knows that it's one thing to create a garden, but quite another to maintain it in pristine condition. So how large was Francis's team? Mrs Lybbe Powys informs us that 'Fifty men are constantly employ'd in keeping the pleasure-grounds, rides, &c., in order, in all about 1000 acres'. The 2000 *National Trust Guidebook* also states there were fifty gardeners: 'A team of 50 gardeners, supervised by the steward, Francis Faugoin, were kept busy looking after the garden.' Today, the Head Gardener manages five full-time gardeners and two part-time, assisted by twenty-five volunteers.

We do know the names of two of the gardeners who worked for Francis: Richard Wood and Bartholemew (Bat) Lapham.

Richard Wood was a witness to Francis's will, made in 1787, the year before Francis died. Richard Wood is not to be confused with Richard Woods, whose nursery in Chertsey is referred to later. Wood was born in 1748, married at Great Bedwyn in 1777 aged twenty-nine, and his first child was baptised in Stourton church later that year. He may well have started working in the garden as a young boy of fifteen, but if we take 1777 as a start date, it still means he worked alongside Francis from 1777 until 1787 – a full ten years. After Francis died, Wood continued to work for Richard Colt Hoare until 1821 – a further thirty-three years. This gives a total of forty-three years. Wood was obviously good at his job and a trusted servant for Colt Hoare. Jean found a poster in some papers at the Wiltshire & Swindon History Centre. It stated:

> Five Guineas Reward. Whereas a considerable quantity of Fruit, Potatoes Cabbages and other Vegetables have at different times been stolen and taken away from the Gardens and Grounds of Sir Richard Hoare Bart. of Stourhead. Notice is hereby given that the above Reward of Five Guineas will be given on the Conviction of the Offenders, by me Richard Wood, Gardener.

He must have been in a position of some authority to have his name on the poster, which, unfortunately, is not dated.

Bartholemew Lapham (1771–1835) was another long-serving gardener. He was born in Stourton and started working in the garden in 1784 as a lad of thirteen. Henry had moved to Clapham by 1784, so Bat was employed by Colt Hoare and may have trained initially under Francis, who was sixty-eight when Bat started work. Writing in the Annals in 1835, Colt Hoare said: 'Bat Lapham, my old gardener of 50 years, died.' Bat is buried in Stourton churchyard. Colt Hoare ceased writing the Annals in 1835.

John Evil is the only other name we know who was contemporary with Francis. He's mentioned in the 1782 letter from Francis to Henry asking for instructions about the 'Cottage by the Pantheon':

> ... John Evil has been saying there [sic] will want a shed by the Necessary house
> for him to put a little wood in the dry, one may be put there out of sight of
> the Garden ...

The 'Necessary house' was the outside privy. Francis took care to sight the shed (and presumably the privy) out of the sight of visitors to the garden. The Evil family had lived in Stourton for generations: Jean found a baptism in 1606.

So, what were Francis and his team of gardeners planting and growing in the garden?

In his book, *Early Nurserymen*,[10] John Harvey states that the earliest priced catalogues did not appear until 1775, well after the Stourhead garden was finished. Figures for what was available and how much was paid, therefore, must be gleaned from contemporary accounts of other large estates. One such estate was that of Hartwell House in Buckinghamshire; today, this beautiful house and grounds is a luxury hotel managed by the Historic House Hotels group in partnership with the National Trust. Hartwell House was the ancestral home of Sir William Lee, Bt (1726–1799). He purchased trees, shrubs and pineapple plants from Richard Woods, nurseryman of Chertsey in Surrey. An account submitted by Woods shows the wide range of plants stocked in his nursery and, usefully for our purposes, gives the numbers supplied and the cost in 1759,[11] the year contemporary with completion of the Pantheon.

Woods' total bill for the year was £148 17s 11d. A small selection of the range and variety of plants Woods could supply included a hundred each of beech, hornbeam, fine young oaks and 'plain hollys', and fifty 'Lyburnums'. Eighteen years after John Faugoin was asked where a laburnum could be procured, they were now easily available, and in quantity. Woods was also able to provide fifty succession pineapple plants at two shillings and sixpence each, and forty fruiting pines at seven shillings each. Woods went on to become a garden designer and this same account included a 'Design for a New Garden Greenhouse and Pinery', at a cost of twelve guineas. This significant sum of money shows the value of Francis's expertise when advising Lord Bruce on the design of his pineapple house, and the value of the plants that Henry supplied to Lord Bruce.

Other similar nurseries had sprung up around London. The village of Chelsea was sited outside the city on the banks of the Thames, where the soil was extremely fertile. Sir Hans Sloane, who lived at Cheyne Manor close by the river, leased an area of this fertile land to the Royal Society of Apothecaries in perpetuity: the Chelsea Physic Garden. There were many tree nurseries and market gardens producing every kind of vegetable and fruit needed for the hungry citizens.

We can get an idea of the cost of some of these fruit plants from another early nurseryman, Henry Clark of Chipping Campden, Gloucestershire. Clark supplied the Norton estates of Sir Dudley Ryder (1691–1756) as gardener and steward.[12] His 1753 account included dwarf pears, peaches, nectarines, 'apricocks', Morello cherries and 'greaps'. The pears were one shilling each, the peaches, apricots and nectarines one shilling and sixpence each, and three 'greaps' one shilling and sixpence.

Francis would surely have made use of these suppliers. He would no doubt also have made good use of his Quintinye book. His fruit garden must have looked beautiful: highly decorative as well as productive.

Walking round the garden, it's easy to forget that the wonderful trees we see today were never seen by Francis and Henry, because so many of them were later introductions. The magnificent North American redwoods, for example, and the Asiatic magnolias and rhododendrons had not yet arrived in England from those far-flung corners of the globe. The American *Magnolia grandiflora*, however, was an earlier introduction and first flowered in London in August 1737 in the Parsons Green garden of Sir Charles Wager, First Lord of the Admiralty. The famously skilled botanical artist, Georg Dionysius Ehret (1708–1770), walked every day from his home in Chelsea to Parsons Green, Fulham, to watch the magnolia bloom and to paint every stage from bud to full flowering.

An even earlier introduction from the Appalachian Mountains in eastern North America – the tulip tree (*Liriodendron tulipifera*) – was first seen in the forests of Virginia by John Tradescant the younger on his second trip to North America, and was introduced in England around 1688. The largest and oldest example of this tree at Stourhead today is by the side of the lake just beyond the entrance to Rock Arch and was planted by Richard Colt Hoare in 1792.

It would seem likely, therefore, that Henry may well have purchased some of these trees for planting by Francis and his team.

Nonetheless, to our eyes, the garden in the 18th century would seem to offer a restricted palette. But Henry did have the native trees – the broadleaves, beech, oak, ash and sycamore – and these he and Francis planted in quantity. Henry had only a few conifers at his disposal: larch, common or Norway spruce and yew.

And, of course, Cedar of Lebanon. This was another must-have tree for the owners of large estates and parkland, introduced around 1630 or 1640. Henry would have seen these trees at the Chelsea Physic Garden, where four trees were planted at the entrance. Ehret illustrated one of these for his friend, Philip Miller, curator of the garden. The Stourhead cedar is a rather battered old tree, not at all representative of the majestic, wide-spreading cedars of other estates. Did Henry plant it? It is certainly precious to the garden team today because it is such an old specimen. They carry out careful pruning where necessary and the Trust has spent a large sum on having the tree X-rayed to make sure that there is no internal deterioration.

The underplanting of common laurel was begun by Henry and greatly increased by Colt Hoare. This was a good choice: very few plants will grow successfully under beech (except bluebells), and the laurel gives a beautiful, textured understorey, reflecting the sunlight on its shiny, evergreen leaves. However, it's not such a good choice for the gardeners, whose job it is to prune them every year – a mammoth, back-breaking task.

Henry expressed his ideas on planting trees by saying:

> The greens should be arranged in large masses as the shades are in painting, to contrast the *dark* masses with the *light* ones, and to relieve each dark mass itself with little sprinklings of lighter greens here and there.[13]

These instructions demonstrate his painterly eye, but they aren't much practical help to Francis, who has the task of turning Henry's vision into reality. To do this, Francis would need to decide which varieties of tree to use and how many of each variety would be required, and to calculate the necessary spacing. Fortunately for Henry, Francis was more than capable of making these decisions.

Stourhead's tree collection is a historic one. Over the years, it has reflected the many additions planted by the Hoare family, and by the National Trust. Some trees have died of old age, disease or storm damage; others have flourished magnificently. Henry and Francis would have been astonished at the size and variety on display.

As any gardener knows, it's not possible to discuss the growth of the trees and plants without considering the weather. As a keen gardener for most of my adult life, I know how much we gardeners like to talk about the weather. Will it be a fine spring with light showers, encouraging the plants to grow and the fruit to set, or a cold one that will hold back the unfurling leaves on the trees and the greening of the hedges? Will we have a cold, hard winter, or a long, hot summer? While researching the chronology of the creation of the garden, I've often wondered, 'What was the weather like when the Pantheon was being built, or the lake created?' Was the weather a help or a hindrance? I discovered that the years when the greatest amount of building activity took place at Stourhead, 1750 to 1760, had ten wet summers in a row. The summers in this period were the wettest in a record that began in 1697, with 1751 being regarded as a notably wet year. Such bad weather didn't seem to slow down the pace of work, however: by 1760, the Grotto, wooden Palladian bridge, Pantheon and lake were all completed.

From 1763 until 1772 (Temple of Apollo, Stone Bridge, Alfred's Tower), the wet summers continued. But they were also warm, with the exception of the hot summer of 1765. In a letter to his daughter, Susanna, dated July 1765, Henry tells her that 'Dear Harriot dives like a Di Dapper & there is no keeping Her out of the Water this Hissing Hot Weather'.[14] A 'Di Dapper' was the country name for a Little Grebe. A letter to Lord Bruce,[15] a month later in August that year, states:

> ... We never were so put to it to keep cool in this House. We dine with the Hall Doors open into the Stair Case which We never did before for the Door into the Air would let in the Heat of a Firey Furnace.

After a dip in the cool waters of the Grotto, he continues:

> ... Next I ride under the spreading Beaches [sic] just beyond the Obelisk on the Terrace where We are sure of Wind and Shade & a delightfull View into the Vale....

The hot summer was followed by a severe winter, the cold weather starting in November 1765 and continuing until February the following year. The years 1766, 1767 and 1768 all started with a bitterly cold January, with severe frosts. Although I wanted to know how the weather affected the builders and the gardeners, when reading Henry's letters, it became apparent that uppermost in Henry's mind was how the weather affected the crops – particularly the wheat. On 31st August 1768, Henry reported to Lord Bruce:[16]

> ... I never felt such severe Cold in August before. Thank God the Weather has been fine ever since & the Wheat is universally in about Us ... We have heard nothing all this Drip^g Sum^r but what a Short Crop rainy Seasons always produce ... But thanks to the Allmighty Good God it turns out beyond all expectation & The Tears of the Poor I hope will now by dryd up ...

He adds a footnote to the letter: 'The Crops of Barley, Oats, Beans & peas are equal to the Wheat.'

Henry knew how much food shortages affected poor people. On Boxing Day that year, Henry wrote to Lord Bruce and told him:

> ...the Poor are turned Thieves nothing escapes Them. They have 4 Times attempted My Larder & succeeded Twice, Cheese, Beef, Veal & Pork in Pickle was all cleared. ... Hunger will break thro' Stone Walls, it is plain.[17]

These comments are a sobering reminder that starvation was never far away. I came to realise that coping with bad weather when creating the garden was trivial by comparison and was reminded that we should be thankful for the year-round availability of food today.

1 Ailesbury archive. Wiltshire & Swindon History Centre, Chippenham. WSA 9/35/53.
2 Ibid. WSA 9/35/53.
3 Dodd, Dudley, ed. *The Letters of Henry Hoare 1760–81.* Wiltshire Record Society, Wiltshire & Swindon History Centre, Chippenham, 2018. p. 91. WSA 9/35/165(1)/1426.
4 Campbell, Susan. *A History of Kitchen Gardening.* Frances Lincoln Ltd, London, 2005. p. 159
5 Ibid. p. 164.
6 *Journal of Garden History.* Vol. 23, No. 2. Winter 1995. pp. 246–249.
7 http://lwlimages.library.yale,edu/strawberyyhill/oneitem.asp.id=153
8 *Parson Woodforde Society Journal.* Vol. VI. No. 1. Spring 1973. p. 12.
9 Dodd, Dudley, ed. *The Letters of Henry Hoare 1760–1781.* Wiltshire Record Society 2018. p. 132. WSA 9/35/165(2)/1478.
10 Harvey, John. *Early Nurserymen.* Phillimore & Co. Ltd, 1974.
11 Ibid. Appendix XI, 'Shrubs, Roses, Pines & Vines 1755–1770'. pp. 202—207.
12 Ibid. Appendix VIII. 'Henry Clerk of Chipping Campden, Gloucestershire'. pp. 191–193.
13 Woodbridge, Kenneth. *The Stourhead Landscape.* National Trust Guide Book, 2002. p. 61.
14 Dodd, Dudley, ed. *The Letters of Henry Hoare 1760–1781.* Wiltshire Record Society 2018. p. 83. WSA 9/35/165(1)/1117.
15 Ibid. p. 85. WSA 1300/3264.
16 Ibid. p. 112. WSA 9/35/165(1)/-.
17 Ibid. p. 118. WSA 9/35/165(1)/1480.

CHAPTER FIFTEEN

A LIVING WORK
OF ART

HENRY MUST HAVE been happy with the result of ten long years of thought, planning and effort. He had a good team. His choice of Henry Flitcroft to design the Temple of Ceres, the Temple of the Nymph and the Temple of Hercules had been a good one; the two men had enjoyed a mutually beneficial working relationship. Privett had proved his worth as a skilled and reliable stonemason.

And Francis had marshalled the workforce and helped to overcome the inevitable problems as they arose.

Standing on the Pantheon steps, Henry could look across the wide expanse of water towards the church and village in the distance. But he felt that something else was needed. We know this because of a letter he wrote to his daughter Susanna. He'd clearly explained his ideas to her, and she'd made the suggestion that helped to provide the answer. In his letter of 23rd October 1762, he writes that he has followed her instructions and enthusiastically describes his plans:[1]

> ... the Stone Bridge of 5 Arches. You always wish'd I would build at the passage
> into the orchard & the scheme of carrying the Water up & loosing out of sight
> towards the parish. This Bridge is now about. It is simple and plain. I took it
> from Palladio's Bridge at Vicenza, 5 arches & when You stand at the pantheon
> the Water will be seen thro the Arches & it will look as if The River came down
> thro the Village & that this was the Village Bridge for publick use. The View of
> the Bridge, Village & Church altogether will be a Charm^g Gasp^d picture at the
> end of that Water.

He continues by saying that Privett's estimate for carriage of his better-quality stone is £53, but 'The Arches I turn with my rough Stone'. Presumably, Privett then built the bridge. The building of this second Palladian bridge completed the circular walk and echoed the same design detail as the first Palladian bridge.

Henry had a faultless eye and placed this bridge in exactly the right position. By making the water appear to disappear out of sight towards the village when viewed from the Pantheon steps, it had the effect of disguising the boundary of the lake.

Today, the effect seems obvious: smooth grass surrounds the bridge and leads the eye on to the Bristol Cross and the church beyond. But in 1762, when Henry was planning this bridge, the area was occupied by an orchard – and it is likely he had not yet seen the Bristol Cross.

Always planning further improvements, Henry was clearly delighted to see how much the position of the stone bridge enhanced the view when seen from the Pantheon. But there was another problem. The public road from Stourton village to Gasper cut through his property, passing close to the side of the new lake. The everyday traffic of farm carts, carriages and coaches could be seen. He had no wish to prevent local people and travellers going about their daily business; but how could he take visitors across the road and, without realising it, briefly out of the garden, before progressing on up the hillside to the next highlight? Then there was the difficulty of bringing people back down the hill and into the garden again.

Why take visitors out of the garden at all? Because Henry was planning his next project. The ground rose sharply on this side of the valley, and he realised that a temple placed on the crown of the hill would be the perfect vantage point to look down over the entire garden. He might well have recalled his visit to Lake Nemi. As we know, he had purchased a painting of Nemi from Richard Wilson four years earlier, in 1758. Perhaps this painting gave him a model for his next bold plan. He would build a temple dedicated to Apollo – the twin brother of Diana – high on the hillside, looking down on his newly formed lake.

Henry also purchased another important painting that same year. When visiting Florence, he became acquainted with the Envoy Extraordinary there, Horace Mann (1706–1786). Mann was a point of contact for English Grand Tourists arriving in Florence. He was well known and hospitable, and acted as an agent, negotiating purchases of art for wealthy English visitors.

On Henry's behalf, Mann bought a painting by Carlo Maratta (1625–1713) from the Pallavicini family. This painting must surely have been even more of an inspiration for the Temple of Apollo; it celebrates the notable reputation of the wealthy Niccolò Maria Pallavicini, built on his encouragement of art in Rome. It's a huge painting and shows the Temple of Virtù sitting atop a steep hillside, approached by a zig-zag path. Apollo is indicating the route. Intriguingly, it also shows a self-portrait of the artist appearing to be in the act of painting a portrait of Pallavicini: a painting within a painting.

The plan to build another eye-catching temple was an exciting one. But the difficulty remained: how to gain access to the temple across the road? Henry may well then have had a flash of inspiration: perhaps he remembered how this exact same problem was solved at his house at Quarley. The garden there was divided from the house by the village road. To gain access from one side of the garden to the other, a brick tunnel had been built under the road, while a small bridge carried traffic over the top of the tunnel.

Marchese Niccolò Maria Pallavicini guided to the Temple of Virtù by Apollo with a Self-portrait of the Artist
CARLO MARATTA (1625–1713) | Oil painting on canvas | 1705 | © National Trust Images

Susanna Hoare, Countess of Ailesbury

ARTHUR POND (c.1700-1758) | Oil painting on canvas | 1757 | © National Trust Images

Henry may have realised that he could employ the same principle, slightly altered, to suit the needs of this site.

As this configuration had to be part of the overall plan for the garden, it had to be eye-catching, causing comment and giving enjoyment. The ingenious design disguised the bridge as a rocky arch that allowed traffic to pass underneath it while, at the same time, leading visitors over the arch and up to the Temple of Apollo by means of steep steps and a winding path. Moreover, the execution of the design hid from view the road below. Visitors would not realise they were briefly leaving the garden as their attention was focussed on the difficult climb ahead. Having viewed the Temple of Apollo, visitors would then gain access to the garden again through a tunnel called the Souterrain.

Henry turned to Flitcroft to bring his vision to reality. Flitcroft had almost certainly designed the Grotto; it seems likely, therefore, that he adapted Henry's plan to suit this new purpose by copying its rocky exterior.

Having passed over the dam, the footpath continues by the side of the lake to the base of what, at first sight, appears to be the entrance to a gloomy cave, but is, in fact, the beginning of the route to the Temple of Apollo. Huge boulders form the arched entrance, and moss-covered stones create a damp and dank atmosphere, with ferns sprouting out of the crevices. On entering, steep steps wind up to the right, then left and right again, zigzagging up the hill, passing several false 'caves' on each side, adding to the mystery. It takes quite an effort to climb up: the steps are steep and uneven. The path continues to zigzag up the hillside, until one finally emerges onto a footpath with a more secure footing – the same feeling as was created when climbing up out of the Grotto.

This stroke of inspiration also satisfied Henry's desire to maintain the illusion of being in another world, without any distractions from the real one. He had done the same thing with the wooden Palladian bridge, another imaginative solution to a practical problem.

Having achieved this difficult ascent, the visitor had a clear path to the Temple of Apollo.

Flitcroft's design was based on the famous Syrian Temple of Venus at Baalbec. In 1757 the traveller and scholar, Robert Wood, published *The Ruins of Baalbec*. Henry owned a copy, and he took the design of Apollo from a plate in the book. The temple also has similarities to the Temple of the Sun at Kew, designed by the architect William Chambers, completed in 1761. According to the Rev. Richard Warner, writing in 1801, 'a large cast of the Belvedere Apollo occupies the interior'. This lead statue was originally placed on a mound at the end of the south lawn and was moved to the Temple by Richard Colt Hoare. A fire in the roof in 1837 probably melted the lead statue.

Most other gardens of the period placed eye-catching features at the end of a long walk, or perhaps a canal. The idea was to give a clear, uninterrupted approach. At Stourhead, it's not possible to walk directly to any of the temples. Henry was showing something of interest in the distance, but not showing how to get there; it was a voyage of discovery. All the temples in the garden are approached obliquely and come as a surprise, suddenly looming up in front of you. There are so many little subtleties in the design.

When a visitor takes the circular route around the lake, the sightlines crisscross and the eye can travel seamlessly from one temple to the other. It's Henry's originality of vision that distinguishes Stourhead from other gardens of the time. It was entirely his own interpretation of the 'new' style of garden layout. What emerges is a design like no other. The fact that this garden is the work of a London banker – rather than a professional landscape designer – makes the achievement all the more astonishing.

The steep climb up the hillside to the Temple of Apollo is worth all the effort. As we stand on the steps of Apollo, the whole glorious view spreads out below: the Stone Bridge, the Bristol Cross, the Temple of Flora, the Grotto and the Pantheon, with the calm, reflective waters of the lake at its centre. As Horace Walpole said, this vantage point forms one of the 'most picturesque views in the world'.

Another visitor to the garden was Joseph Spence (1699–1798), an historian, Oxford don and friend of Alexander Pope. In September 1765, he gave a report of his visit to his friend the ninth Earl of Lincoln, Henry Pelham-Clinton. He referred to:

> ... an odd sort of ruinous Building which hides the road; and over which you
> wind by roughish steps toward the Walk of the Muses and the Temple of
> Apollo ... The Door, exactly faces the Palladian Bridge; and from it you take in
> all the chief Beauties of the place. It is to be lighted from the top of the Dome;
> & Guido's Aurora ... is to be painted round the inside walls by Mr. Hoare.

The mention of 'Guido's Aurora' refers to the famous large ceiling painting *L'Aurora*, by Guido Reni, for the Casino, or garden house, at the Palazzo Pallavicini in Rome. The beautiful painting shows Aurora (Dawn) leading Apollo in his chariot, bringing sunlight to the world.

In the event, the idea of a fresco round the walls didn't materialise. Neither did the Walk of the Muses. What a pity; both would have been appropriate. Apollo was the leader of the Muses, representing the arts, science, music, comedy and tragedy, poetry, and dance.

However, the artist William Hoare of Bath did paint a version of Aurora on the back of a bench, curved to fit the wall of the temple. In his interpretation, as well as drawing on Reni's picture, William Hoare referenced Poussin's painting *Dance to the Music of Time*, which shows Aurora and Apollo in the sky above. Both paintings were sources for the beautiful painting on the bench. This bench is no longer displayed in the Temple of Apollo but is safely in store in the house.

Henry liked to be seen to be in the forefront of fashion and to create enjoyable 'interludes' to charm his visitors. One such 'interlude' is the cascade below the lake. In 1765, the same year that the Temple of Apollo was finished, Henry discussed with his friends, Bampfylde and William Hoare, the idea of creating a cascade. Bampfylde was

The Temple of Apollo overlooking the lake at Stourhead, Wiltshire, | © National Trust Images/Chris Lacey

creating a garden at his home, Hestercombe, near Taunton, at the same time as Henry was creating Stourhead. The Hestercombe garden was also set in a valley. From a spring-fed pond, Bampfylde constructed a brick-built leat, over three hundred yards long, to carry water to the head of the Great Cascade. In a letter dated 23rd December 1765, Henry expressed his delight:

> Messrs. Bampfield and Hoare have made me an ingenious model for the Cascade like Mr. Bampfields & as I have a Stone Quarr on the Hill just above it, I hope to finish it soon in the Summer.[2]

Henry's cascade carried water from the lake through a large pipe under the road to a brick-built arch, where it poured over a stone slab down into the river below. When viewed from ground level, it's apparent that the large boulders were carefully placed to create maximum effect: the water gushes and tumbles in all directions, sparkling in the sunlight. Henry later purchased a painting of Mr Bampfylde's cascade by John Inigo Richards, and today this painting hangs in the house in the South Apartment.

Other 'interludes' in Henry's design were removed by Colt Hoare, including the Turkish Tent and the Gothic Greenhouse, both in place around the time the Temple of Apollo was being constructed. (Detailed descriptions are given in Appendix II.)

Henry added one finishing touch to the picture he was creating. On a mound between the church and the stone bridge, he erected the Bristol High Cross. He had come across this medieval cross when visiting his friend, Cutts Barton, who was Dean of Bristol Cathedral.

The High Cross was a market cross, erected in Bristol around 1400. It stood in the centre of the town, at the crossroads of its four main streets: High Street, Broad Street, Corn Street and Wine Street. Four tiers of decreasing height feature statues of English monarchs. Through the centuries, the High Cross had served as a rallying point for ceremonies and notable events. It had fallen into disrepair, however, and the local citizens requested its removal, fearing its imminent collapse. A fund was raised to re-site the cross in Bristol on College Green, but once again it was eventually viewed as an obstruction; it was taken down and 'was thrown by in a corner of the Cathedral, where it lay for a long while neglected'. This is where Henry first saw it.

It was a serendipitous encounter. Henry had begun to appreciate the Gothic style, and in June 1763 visited Strawberry Hill, Horace Walpole's home by the Thames at Twickenham. The term 'Gothic' was given to the re-interpretation of medieval architecture and design; the style was gaining in popularity. In a letter to Lord Bruce, Henry commented:

> I was highly entertained at Mr. Walpole's last Saturday with the finest painted Glass Windows & Gothick Taste in the best manner that it can be employ'd in so small a Space.[3]

A letter to Harriot | letter dated 18th July 1776 | Image courtesy Wiltshire and Swindon History Centre

Henry knew the perfect place to display the cross in the garden. He asked his friend, the Dean, if he could take it away. He wrote to the Bristol architect, Thomas Paty, for advice on the best method of repairing and supporting the cross, and informed him:

> The Dean of Bristol is so obliging as to write to me word I may now send for the Cross directly. I have therefore ordered my servant Faugoin, to send out two waggons from Stourhead ...

It was transported to Stourhead in October 1764, but not erected until December the following year. Henry wrote to Lord Bruce on 23rd December 1765:

> I also saw the first Story of the Cross put just together & repair'd & now the rest will go on swimmingly & be done sooner than We expected & the foundation of Stones is finished & the mount forming round it & also round the Temple of Apollo.[4]

Henry's delight and sense of humour once again comes shining through in another letter to Lord Bruce, also dated December 1765:

> The Cross is now in hand & there are so many pieces that We must I believe employ Harriot to put it together as She is such an Adept in joyning the map of the Countys of England.[5]

Harriot was eleven years old at the time.

The High Cross was originally painted bright colours: red, blue and gold. Vestiges of paint remained on the stone figures. Eleven years after erecting the cross at Stourhead, Henry repainted it in the original vivid colours and completed the refurbishment with a golden ball and iron cross atop the pinnacle. A painting by Bampfylde at Hestercombe shows these bright colours. A letter dated 11th May 1776 to Lord Bruce describes the great pleasure Henry had in showing his grandchildren round the garden:

> Thank God they are all fine & well & now make nothing of walking round the Gardens & I mounted The Tower Thursday with the Dear Children & They are vastly delighted with this spot ... The Cross now new painted fills Them with rapture.[6]

A letter to Harriot dated 18th July 1776 is positively gleeful when describing the reaction it caused when viewed by the locals.

> ... it is wonderful what Crowds of [Country (*inserted*)] People go to Court here. The Kings & Queens all so richly robed in Cloth of Gold, Ermine ...[7]

However, not everyone was quite so enraptured. Once again, Mrs Lybbe Powys paints a vivid picture – and is vociferous in her dislike:

> The first building after the gardener's cottage is the Bristol Cross... but its kings and queens in the niches round it would, in my opinion, have look'd better in the original stone colour than so ornamented with red, blue and gilt clothing; but still 'tis pretty enough through this profusion of finery, and I believe, it may in some measure be more strikingly gaudy from its nearness to one. Could it be plac'd on an eminence at a little distance, it surely would have a more pleasing effect.[8]

Mrs Powys was clearly not well versed when it came to historical accuracy; medieval statues were frequently painted very bright colours. The elaborate decoration on the west front of Wells Cathedral, for example, was a blaze of colour: the painted statue of the Virgin Mary was set against a bright blue backdrop, embellished with gold stars.

Today, the four standing figures of kings on the Bristol High Cross are carved stone replicas. The originals are on loan to the V&A, where they stand in niches on the staircase to the left of the main entrance. There, protected from the weather, some vestiges of paint are preserved and the colours can still be seen.

The acquisition of the Bristol Cross signalled a shift of interest for Henry, from Roman history to English history. In quick succession followed two more Gothic features: St Peter's Pump, and the Convent. They were to become features on a ride around the estate – another of Henry's offerings to visitors.

The Convent was a small cottage situated in the woods on the estate. It would have served as a stopping-off point on the wider circuit. Whether on a gallop or a carriage ride, visitors could have used the Convent for shelter and perhaps refreshments. Originally a building of two rooms downstairs and two upstairs, the design is quirkily rustic and Gothic combined. A thatched roof covers an asymmetric building. The walls are studded with large, fist-sized, lumps of stone, reminiscent of the Grotto or Rock Arch. Pointed Gothic windows and doors add to the effect. The tall chimneys and spires are all different, towering above the roof. Inside, twelve small niches in the walls once contained painted wooden panels depicting nuns.

When Sir John Parnell, the Chancellor of the Irish Exchequer, visited in 1769, he mentioned that '... The Convent (called the Abbey) was occupied by a man and his wife who bred fine wild turkeys, bantam fowl and guinea hens'.

The Convent still exists, and today is a private residence. Anne and I were lucky enough to be invited to visit by the then owner. We were as amused and delighted by its appearance as 18th-century visitors must have been.

The growing interest in Gothic soon took on overtones of patriotism. Henry's interest in English history led him back to the father of the nation: Alfred the Great. The estate was reputed to include the location where Alfred raised his standard and mustered his forces from Somerset, Wiltshire and Hampshire before marching on to meet the Danes in the decisive battle at Ethandun. This rallying point was called Kingsettle Hill, and it was here that Henry decided to build Alfred's Tower.

My interest, too, in Alfred and the battle of Ethandun had now come full circle, when I realised that Alfred's Tower at Stourhead was such a prominent feature in the wider landscape.

The last feature, which is missing from the garden today, was the Hermitage. Built around the time Alfred's Tower was completed, it was placed on the hilltop near to the Temple of Apollo. The design echoed the layout of the Grotto and was imaginatively constructed of upturned tree roots with an entrance and a central chamber. The Hermitage attracted many comments from visitors and was much admired. (Details are given in Appendix II.)

Throughout, I have referred to 'the garden', but in the 18th century it would have been called the Pleasure Grounds. This, after all, is exactly what it did – it gave pleasure. Visitors at that time would have distinguished between the Pleasure Grounds and the wider estate, and they were as impressed by the outer circuit as by the garden itself.

When Parnell visited in 1769, he recounts his delight at discovering the ride from the Obelisk along Terrace Ride to Alfred's Tower, returning down the valley past the Convent and St Peter's Pump. At the date of his visit, Alfred's Tower was unfinished. He writes:

> Here is about building a belvedere which will cost a vast sum. It is to be
> dedicated to Alfred who it is imagin'd in the adjoining wood used to hold his
> councils. It is triangular with three towers ...
>
> This kind of drive on the brow of a hill dressd smooth about the breadth of
> a race-course is one of the most striking and pleasing of all the improvements,
> affording a charming place for air and exercise any time of the year taking in
> the beauties of the surrounding country and giving a place the appearance of the
> greatest extent.

With the erection of Alfred's Tower, Henry could justifiably feel satisfied with his efforts. It had taken twenty years. His great passion for art and architecture, coupled with his unique vision, had culminated in the creation of a landscape 'painting' comparable with the great artists he so admired. In fact, arguably, he had surpassed these artists: his 'painting' was three-dimensional. It was possible to walk in it and through it, the real world and the imaginary world constantly intermingling. This aspect of the design was admired by contemporary visitors, who appreciated the finer points of nature and artifice combining.

Stourhead had become, and remains, a living work of art.

But I had always wondered: How much did this 'living work of art' cost? As stated earlier we know that Henry paid for it from his own pocket and the amounts he paid to the artists and craftsmen. But how much money – in cash – did Henry give to Francis to create the Pleasure Grounds? And how much to pay the labourers and gardeners, to purchase trees and plants, and to provide a wage for himself.

I totalled all the sums recorded in the ledgers, beginning in 1747 with the first payment to Francis at Stourhead and ending with the last payment in 1783. These figures speak volumes for the trust invested in Francis and give just a small idea of the enormity of the task. But the total amount of money is not small.

I give below the breakdown of the figures and how they relate to the various stages of the garden's development. There may be some omissions and overlaps but as far as possible they follow the entries in the ledgers.

PAYMENTS TO FRANCIS FAUGOIN FROM HENRY HOARE'S PERSONAL LEDGERS, 1747–1783

1747–1756	Grotto; Obelisk; Wooden Palladian Bridge; Dam; Lake; Pantheon	£9,336
1757–1768	Completion of Pantheon; Stone Bridge; Rock Arch & Souterrain; Temple of Apollo; Bristol Cross; Cascade; Convent; St. Peter's Pump; Alfred's Tower	£32,052
1769–1773	Completion of Tower and Hermitage	£7,155
TOTAL AMOUNT OF CASH GIVEN TO FRANCIS FAUGOIN:		**£48,543**

1 Dodd, Dudley, ed. *The Letters of Henry Hoare 1760–1781*. Wiltshire Record Society 2018, p. 43. WSA 1300/4280.
2 Ibid. p. 94. WSA 9/35/165(1)/1109.
3 Ibid. p. 65. WSA 9/35/165(1)/2408.
4 Ibid. p. 94. WSA 9/35/165(1)/1109.
5 Ibid. p. 92. WSA 9/35/165(1)1426.
6 Ibid. p. 152. WSA 1300/2948.
7 Ibid. p. 163. WSA 9/35/165(1)/3192.
8 Powys, C. Passages from the *Diaries of Mrs. Philip Lybbe Powys of Hardwick House*, Oxford, 1756–1808. ed. E.J. Climenson, 1899.

Anne Hoare, Mrs Richard Hoare playing a Cittern (after Francis Cotes)
SAMUEL WOODFORDE, RA (1763-1817)
Oil painting on canvas | after 1757 | © National Trust Images

CHAPTER SIXTEEN
FAMILIES

⁂

DURING THE TEN years between 1755, when the dam was completed, and 1765, when Apollo was finished, both Henry and Francis experienced important family events. Henry's much-loved younger daughter, Anne, married her cousin, Richard, on 20th March 1756. Sadly, their first son, Henry Richard, was born and buried a year later. A second son, baptised on 9th December 1758, they named Richard Colt: Richard for his father and great-great grandfather, and Colt from his grandmother's maiden name, Susan Colt. There must have been great rejoicing, not only in the Hoare family, but also among the Faugoins. Anne would have had a special bond with them both. As she had lived with Francis and Mary for almost nine months after the death of her mother, she must have seemed like a daughter to Mary.

Sadly, this joy was not to last. At the age of only twenty-two, Anne died five months after giving birth. Henry's memorial tablet in the church lists all his children but makes special mention of Anne. She must have been very dear to his heart. The memorial states:

> Anne Hoare expired on the 5th May 1759 leaving a lively image of many amiable Virtues Impressed on the Hearts of all who had the happiness of Knowing her gentle and engaging Character.

In a portrait by Samuel Woodforde in the Entrance Hall (opposite), Anne is playing a cittern. The artist has captured just the hint of a shy smile, which you could imagine breaking into peals of laughter at any moment.

Henry already had a granddaughter, Harriot, the daughter of Susanna and Lord Dungarvan. Harriot was three years old when Dungarvan died, and her mother married for a second time, this time to Lord Bruce, later Earl of Ailesbury. On 23rd March 1762, Susanna gave birth to a son, George, a second grandson for Henry. A girl followed a year later, on 1st May 1763: Henry's second granddaughter, named Caroline Anne. A third granddaughter, Frances Elizabeth, was born on 31st May 1765; and another grandson, Charles, in 1767, who only lived for nine months. Susanna gave birth to a much-longed-for third son, another Charles, who was born six years later, in 1773.

Charles, being the baby of the family, was adored by his grandfather. Henry fondly referred many times to 'the dear Charles' in his letters. When Charles was three years old, he gave a lovely description:

The Dear Charles gets stouter every day & is quite a Rantipole. Walked yesterday up to the 6 Wells & back again. I believe soon We shall not find out a Walk long enough for him. He is an Infant Hercules, but the hot Weather seems coming in & that will stop His Speed.[1]

The word 'rantipole' denotes boisterous, unruly behaviour. And it may well have amused Henry to compare Charles with the 'Infant Hercules' who, reputedly, had the strength as a baby to strangle a snake with his bare hands. Two years later, on 27th August 1778:

Charles the well beloved is so stout… & if ever there was a Lovely Child, then He is the one.[2]

For the Faugoin family, 1764 was an important year. Jean was keen to see what more she could discover about their children, particularly Henry, who by that time was twenty-one years of age. She'd done a bit of preliminary research and discovered that Henry Faugoin trained to become a Writer for the Honourable East India Company. She decided that a visit to the British Library would be necessary – and was astonished by the story which began to unfold.

She found several documents, including a certificate from Christ's Hospital School, which was addressed to the Honourable Court of Directors, the East India Company, and stated:

19th September 1764
These are to certify that Henry Faugoin hath gone through a regular course of Book-keeping and Merchants Accounts with me, Thos. Smith.[3]

Christ's Hospital School was commonly known as the Bluecoat School. The nickname 'Bluecoat School' stemmed from the long blue coats worn by pupils; boys wore blue knee-breeches and girls blue pleated skirts, and both wore bright yellow stockings. This distinctive uniform is still worn today.

Christ's Hospital School is one of the oldest boarding schools in England. It was founded in 1552 by King Edward VI and provided food, clothing and an education for orphans and the children of poor families; from the beginning, girls were admitted. Since its establishment, Christ's Hospital has been a charity school with the core aim of offering children from humble backgrounds the chance of a better education, preparing them for future careers. In London, the great majority of children were educated in the Writing School for a position in commerce or trade.

Funded by City businesses and the Church, the school retains its connections with these organisations, some of which have an ancient right to 'Present' a child to the school. Henry was a Governor of Christ's Hospital. *The London Evening Post* of 3rd–6th March 1764 printed 'A list of such Governors of Christ's Hospital, London as are to Present Children at Easter 1764…Henry Hoare Esq., Fleet Street'. So, we may assume that it was probably Henry who 'Presented' the young Henry Faugoin.

Henry Faugoin hoped to be accepted as a Writer by the Honourable East India Company. Young men employed as Writers (clerks) to the Factories (trading posts) kept accounts and were responsible for correspondence with London. Every letter to Head Office was completed in triplicate, to ensure delivery; two copies were sent by two different sailing ships and the third went overland. All senior posts as Writers were obtained by a nomination by the Directors, and these Writers' Petitions (or job applications) had to include baptismal certificates, testimonials and details of education. From 1741, a Bond for faithful service was also required.

The East India Company allowed leeway for creative personal trading, as long as its own profits were not affected. Consequently, a young man who survived ten years in a trying and dangerous climate could be expected to return home a wealthy man. It would have been an attractive prospect for the young Henry Faugoin.

Within two weeks of completing his training, Henry submitted his petition to the Court of Directors.

> The humble petition of Henry Faugoin
>
> That your Petitioner having been educated in writing and accounts humbly hopes he is qualified to serve your Honours abroad.
>
> He therefore humbly prays your Honours would be pleased to admit him a Writer at one of your settlements in the East Indies wherein he promises to behave himself with the greatest Diligence and Fidelity and is ready to give such Security as your Honours shall think proper.
>
> And your Petitioner shall ever pray, Henry Faugoin
>
> Recommended by Christopher Baron
>
> 1st October 1764[4]

By 17th October 1764, the Committee of Correspondence had considered the petitions and concluded that forty-eight Writers were wanted for the Presidencies: fourteen at Fort St George, twenty-six at Bengal and eight at Bombay. Henry's name appeared on the list destined for Bengal.

Jean also found a list of the 'Necessaries for a Writer to India', sold by Welch & Stalker, 134, Leadenhall Street, London. This extensive list hints at the life a Writer might be expected to follow:

> Pillows and bed sheets, towels, white silk hose and cotton hose, coats, breeches, fine hats, waistcoats, pistols, saddle and bridle, stationery, Moorish grammar, Persian grammar, Arabian poetry, tea kettle, candles, tobacco, hamper of wine, tea, coffee and chocolate, soap, shaving powder, hair powder.

Henry now had everything in place to leave the small village of Stourton, where he grew up, for an exciting and daunting sea voyage to India. He could look forward to a new life in Bengal and a promising career with one of the most powerful and successful businesses of the day: the Honourable East India Company. Francis must have been so proud of him.

Henry sailed from the Downs on the merchant East Indiaman *Grenville*. The Downs is an area of sheltered sea off the east Kent coast, near the port of Deal. It was protected on the east by the Goodwin Sands, and on the north and west by the coast. The Downs served as a permanent base for warships patrolling the North Sea and a gathering point for refitted or newly built ships. The *Grenville* was built at the Royal Dockyard at Deptford and launched onto the Thames on 10th December 1764. It had three decks, ninety-nine crew and twenty-six guns, under the command of Captain Parson Fenner. This was its maiden voyage.

Sailing from the Downs on 4th March 1765, the *Grenville* arrived, on 29th March, in Sao Tiago, the largest of the Cape Verde islands, off the west coast of Africa. It rounded the Cape on 5th July, docked at Madras on 5th September, and then sailed on up the east coast of India, docking at Kedgeree on 15th October 1765: seven and a half months after leaving England. Kedgeree was a settlement near the mouth of the River Hooghly, sixty-eight miles from Calcutta. It was well known as the usual anchorage for East Indiamen.

And then Jean found a letter, dated 11th March 1766, to the East India Directors in London. It came from a Company Director in Fort William, a fort and British trading post in Calcutta, named after King William III. The settlement was built during the early years of the Bengal Presidency of British India and sits on the eastern bank of the Hooghly River. The letter brought bad news:

> The writers of last season appointed to this establishment are arrived and have been stationed at different offices except Mr. Faugoing [sic] who died in the passage.[5]

I cannot imagine the pain felt by Francis and Mary on eventually hearing this news: their eldest son, with such a bright future ahead of him, dying of disease on board ship. But I can imagine Henry being a great support to them. It's scarcely credible that Francis and Henry should have suffered in the same way, losing their eldest sons in distressing circumstances far away from home.

Another document stated that:

> ... the length of the voyage has proved fatal to most of her recruits from the scurvey and other distempers which raged among them. ... we immediately ordered all the relief in our power from fresh provisions etc. to be sent down the River to the survivors and we hope most of them will now recover.[6]

The news of Henry Faugoin's death, in fact, did not come as a shock to me and Jean. We'd read, on the Faugoin memorial tablet in the church:

> Henry who died in Calcutta (in the Civil Service of the Honourable East India Company) the 26th May 1765 age 21 years.

But we now knew that he didn't die in Calcutta, but onboard ship, two months after docking at Sao Tiago.

I hoped to unravel a bit more of the story. I contacted the British Library, explaining what we had already learnt about Henry Faugoin but that we would like to know if there were any other papers that might throw further light on the circumstances of his death. A helpful member of the Reference Services department sent a copy of young Henry's will, which made Francis the sole executor, and left all his worldly goods and chattels to him.[7] He instructed Parson Fenner, the Captain, to sell his clothes and linen for a good price and remit in cash or bill the proceeds to his father.

It also stated:

> ... together with the amount of the Bond which is in one of my Chests signed by the said Parson Fenner value Fifty Pounds bearing interest at 8 per cent and payable within Thirty Days after the Arrival of the aforesaid Ship Grenville in Bengall. [sic]
>
> In Witness Whereof I have Hereunto set my Hand and Seal this Twenty Fourth Day of May in the Year of our Lord One Thousand Seven Hundred and Sixty-Five.

There were three Witnesses, one of whom, Isaac Eynard, was also a newly qualified Writer. Although the will is dated 24th May 1765, it wasn't proved until 20th December 1765. We assumed that Henry must have been buried at sea.

It is a moving testament to this young man that, even when seriously ill and close to death, he makes sure his father receives money from the sale of his personal effects, and protects the large amount of silver, provided as a Bond, which is to be returned to his father within thirty days of arrival in Bengal. He shows himself a true Faugoin and a true Huguenot.

Two further documents revealed more information.[8] On 20th November 1765, the Letter Book, which recorded all letters received by the East India Co., stated that the Custom Master in Fort William, Calcutta, was enquiring about a chest of silver 'consigned to Mr Faugoin a writer at this Presidency'. Six years later, enquiries were still being made. By now, the case had been taken up by a Mr Lushington. A letter from him dated 24th February 1771 enquired after the chest of dollars 'belonging to the estate of Mr. Harry Faugoin'. William Lushington had begun his career as a Writer in Bengal, but in 1771 had been promoted to the lucrative post of Factor, allowing him to source and negotiate for goods. I like to think that maybe Mr. Lushington wrote to Francis from Calcutta and returned the money. But we'll never know the sequence of events.

It was sad to realise that Henry's second granddaughter, Frances Elizabeth, was born on 31st May 1765, only five days after the death of Henry Faugoin – before the news had even reached Francis and Mary. The unexpected and devastating loss of young Henry must also have been keenly felt by his younger brothers, Felix and John.

John was Francis's last son to be born and grow up at Stourhead. John became a lawyer and lived in Andover. He died on 25th April 1787, when he was thirty-nine. He is buried alongside Francis and Mary in the churchyard.

Felix was three years younger than Henry and stayed in and around Stourton his whole life. He married Alicia Ford at St Michael's Church in Mere in 1769 when he was twenty-three. They had eight children: one son, Henry, and seven girls: Frances Alicia, Harriot, Sarah, Matilda, Jane, Anne Marie, and Mary Beasley.

Henry, Felix's son, never married. As a result, the Faugoin name disappeared. T.H. Baker, a local historian, recorded:

> The Huguenot family of Faugoin of Stourton, Wiltshire. The last household bearing this patronymic comprised seven daughters renowned for their beauty and one son, but as the son died unmarried, the name is well-nigh forgotten.

How intriguing to read that Francis and Mary had such beautiful granddaughters. I can imagine them walking across the fields from their home, Sarch Farm, to Stourton, to visit their grandparents.

Mary's grandchildren weren't the only ones visiting her. In a letter to Susanna dated 24th May 1776, Henry tells her that 'the dear Charles is as stout as a Buck, has shook off his cold and trudges down to Mary Faugoin's with his waggon twice a day and has found out the easy path to and from it'.[9] It's touching to think that Mary's relationship with Henry's grandchildren was such an easy one; she must have been very loving and kind.

A few months before Felix married, he seemed to have secured good employment working for Henry as manager of Sarch Farm. For eleven years, from 1769 to 1780, he received payment and a gratuity of five guineas for shooting game. But then something went wrong. There's a letter, dated 5th August 1780, which states:

> ... Mr. Webb of Roundhill is now here & We are going over my Farm together & fear I must take what the Faugoins did article for into hand also for They have used me & the Farm allready very ill ...[10]

What happened we'll never know. But it did not seem to create a rift between Francis and Henry. In fact, Felix stayed on at Sarch Farm for another twenty-five years. In 1805, Baker stated 'Mr. Faugoin quitted Sarch Farm, Stourton. His sheep were sold in September.'

This was not the only dispute involving Francis. Two years later, on 23rd December 1782, an entry in the ledger states: 'By Francis Faugoin's dispute with Jane Lloyd concerning the article of oxen and sheep delivered to the House and impossible to be settled but at my loss and expense – £58 13s od.' Jane Lloyd was the housekeeper and must have had an argument with Francis, with both refusing to back down.

Felix, meanwhile, became a churchwarden. He owned various properties in the area, including Horwood House in the nearby town of Wincanton, a coaching stop on the London to Exeter route. He also owned land in the villages of Horsington and Cucklington, and a farm called Snag Farm in Stoke Trister. After leaving Sarch Farm, Felix lived at Wolverton House, together with his only unmarried daughter, Anne Marie, and her sister, Mary Beasley, who was a widow. Felix died in 1825, aged seventy-nine years.

```
            John Faugoin        =        Susannah Le Cerf
             (1666–1743)                    (1680–1757)
```

Charles	John	Elizabeth	Susanna	Jane		Henry
(1702–1739)	(1704–1750)	(1708–)	(1710–)	(1712–)		(1718–1795)

```
                              Francis  =  Mary Swetman
                             (1716–1788)   (1720–1785)
```

Henry		Felix	=	Alicia Ford		John
(1743–1765)		(1746–1825)		(1748–1797)		(1748–1787)

Henry	Frances A	Harriot	Sarah	Matilda	Jane	Anne-Marie	Mary Beasley
(1771–1849)	(1773–1842)	(1775–1848)	(1777–1856)	(1779–1862)	(1782–1827)	(1784–1862)	(1788–1876)

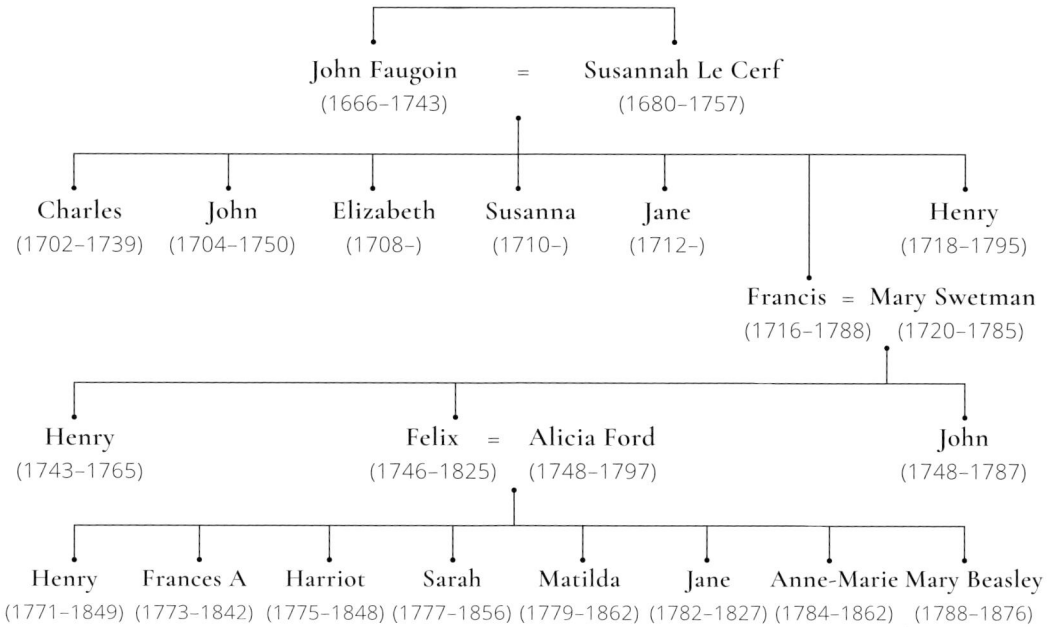

Felix's will[11] revealed that he became relatively wealthy. He left all his estate to his son, Henry, and 'all the rest, residue and remainder of my Household Goods and furniture, family portraits and other pictures, silver and other plate and prints'. He also left a considerable amount of cash to his daughters: £3,900 in total and £30 to each of his grandchildren.

Rather touchingly, he leaves his double-barrel and single-barrel guns to his grandson, Edward Frowd, with the express request that he should 'prise them in remembrance of me'. There are several entries in the Hoare ledger paying Felix for 'game he shot'. He was clearly proud of his skill with a gun and must have passed this on to his grandson.

All in all, then, a large amount of money, land, property and household goods. From my point of view, the most interesting items mentioned in the will are family portraits. Where are these portraits now? Wouldn't we just love to have portraits of Francis and Mary?

Meanwhile, Henry was much preoccupied with the question of his succession.

By 1779, Henry's grandson, Richard Colt, was now old enough to think of marrying. He'd met and become attracted to Hester, the daughter of Sir William Lyttleton. On the face of it, Henry should have been pleased with this turn of events: Sir William's brother, George Lyttleton, was a good friend. He created a famous landscape garden at Hagley Hall that shared many of the features of Stourhead: a temple and a rotunda, a grotto and a hermitage. George Lyttleton moved in political and literary circles; his uncle was Lord Cobham, owner and creator of Stowe. Alexander Pope was a friend.

Richard Colt's attachment to Hester Lyttleton, however, proved problematic. Sir William Lyttleton was a younger son with a smaller inheritance. Hester, therefore, would not bring a large dowry to the marriage.

Henry had always nurtured the hope that Richard Colt would marry Lady Frances, his granddaughter. This expectation had been approved by Henry's daughter, Susanna, Lady Frances's mother. Susanna gave him to understand that she was 'very desirous and anxious that Colt should marry her daughter'. Furthermore, Frances had also intimated that she liked Colt very much and would have been happy with the arrangement. Henry expressed the opinion that he'd made it a rule never to interfere in a 'thing of that sort' and thought 'it was better for young people to choose for themselves'.

However, this state of affairs changed dramatically when Frances formed an attachment to Sir Henry Wilson, a Guards Officer. Everyone was against the match. Her father, Lord Ailesbury, intimated that he would not give her the money she expected to receive as a dowry. However, Frances was determined not to be swayed by the family's objections. And Colt, meanwhile, was equally determined to marry Hester.

Henry could see that there was nothing to be done. In order, as he saw it, to help this situation, Henry devised a plan, which he outlined in his will. And there, he hoped, the matter would rest.

Family situations, however, rarely turn out as expected. Henry was forced to confront the problem again in 1783, when his nephews, Richard – Colt's father – and Fat Harry arrived at Stourhead to discuss the impending marriage of Colt and Hester. Fat Harry wrote a detailed account of this meeting on sixteen loose sheets of paper, which I came across on one of the many visits we made to the Wiltshire & Swindon History Centre.[12]

It made riveting reading. The drama, passion and intensity of feeling expressed, transported me directly to that moment, and into that room. Fat Harry could never have imagined that his neat handwriting on those few sheets of paper could have had such an effect on someone over two hundred years later.

The timing of his nephews' visit could not have been worse. Henry, now aged 78, was in deep mourning for Susanna, his last surviving child, who had died only weeks earlier. To make things even more difficult, Susanna's husband, Lord Ailesbury, was staying at the house. Not only was he grieving for the loss of his wife, but he was also worried about his eldest son, George, who was seriously ill.

The atmosphere was sombre and tense. Understandably, Lord Ailesbury was not in the mood for socialising and stayed in his room, only emerging at mealtimes. Henry did his best to welcome his nephews. The brothers then went for a walk in the garden to discuss their strategy. They thought Henry would be more open with only one person present, so they agreed that Richard was to stay close by and then join Fat Harry and Henry after a little time.

They all met up at tea, avoiding any discussion about Colt and keeping the conversation to small talk. After tea, Harry and Henry were left alone in the room. Henry shut the door. Those few words – 'my Uncle shut the door' – immediately heralded a sense of alarm in me.

Sir Richard Hoare = Susanna Austen
(1648–1718)   (1653–1720)
Founder of Hoare's Bank

Henry L (Good Henry) = Jane Benson
(1677–1724)   (1679–1742)

Henry II ('The Magnificent') = 1 Anne Masham   2 Susan Colt
(1705–1785)   (1708–1727)   (1708–1743)

Anne   Henry   Susanna   Colt   Anne = Richard Hoare
(1727–1735)   (1730–1752)   (1732–1783)   (1733–1740)   (1737–1759)   (1735–1787)

Richard Colt Hoare
(1758–1838)

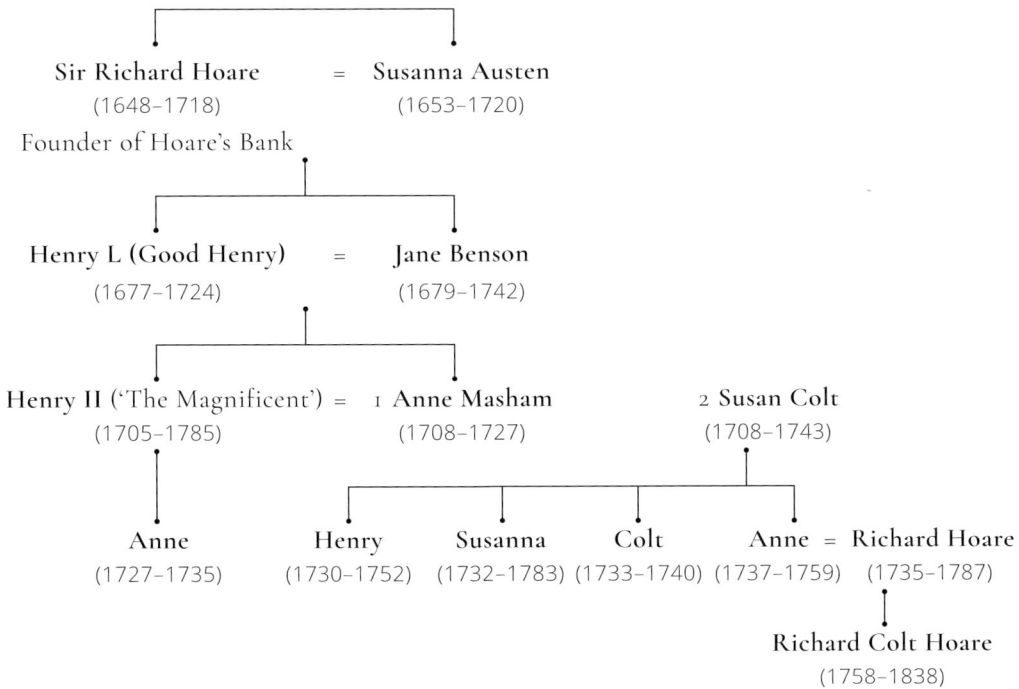

Henry began by saying that he assumed the proposed match was so far advanced that nothing could be done. Harry confirmed that this was the case: all the necessary arrangements were in place, only awaiting the consent of Henry and Sir William. Henry then confided to Harry that he had indeed wished that Colt had formed an attachment to someone with a larger dowry. At this point, Richard came back into the room. Henry, writes Harry, 'desired him to sit down with me' and said that 'he had been thinking over the Business'.

Henry then proceeded to unveil his plan. He wished to bequeath Stourhead to Colt. Both Richard and Harry were taken aback by this news. Richard had expected to inherit Stourhead himself, as the next in line and a Partner at the bank.

Henry then laid out his reasons. He had become increasingly worried about the financial situation in the country: trade was suffering as a result of the American War of Independence (1775–1783) and the political fall-out that followed. Henry feared the collapse of a business that had sustained the family for so many years; come what may, he was determined to safeguard Stourhead.

Worse was to come. His decision to leave Stourhead to Colt was on the proviso that Colt severed all connection with the bank, thus protecting it from any claims by creditors, should the bank fail. This explains why Henry wished Colt to marry an heiress: he knew the Stourhead estate alone wouldn't support the lifestyle he himself had enjoyed, and which he expected Colt would wish to follow. Colt's marriage to Hester – with her limited dowry – presented Henry with a *fait accompli*. So, he had also decided to leave his London properties to Colt, including the bank premises on Fleet Street. These, he reasoned, would provide rental income, which could be added to the income from the country estates, including Stourhead.

As far as Henry was concerned, his plan solved the difficulties of safeguarding Colt's future, whilst at the same time safeguarding his beloved Stourhead.

But his nephews did not see it that way.

At that moment, the bell rang for supper, and everyone went into the dining room. Harry endeavoured to promote a cheerful conversation, but it must have been obvious to everyone that the atmosphere was tense. Henry retired early; Lord Ailesbury and the guests followed suit. The brothers were left to discuss the situation.

Harry recorded: 'We were both so thunderstruck with what had passed, we knew not how or where to begin.' He felt it was '... contrary to Faith, Honor and Justice' and even worse '... Damnd Hypocrisy completed this diabolical Declaration and Transaction for had not the Business we went upon obliged him to confess the Contents of his last Will, ... nothing would have appeared till his Death ...'.

Harry urgently reiterated the dangers of Henry's plan. Not only would his brother, Richard, lose Stourhead and all income from the estate, but the destiny of Hoare's Bank would lie entirely in Colt's hands. He and the other Partners could completely lose their right to decide on the bank's future if Colt so wished it.

Richard appeared to take things more calmly. He said he 'could quietly submit to not enjoying Stourhead and the Estates but would not give up his right to the succession in the Business'.

The brothers agreed to let Harry do the talking next day.

No one slept well that night.

Henry and his nephews met again the following morning. Henry began to explain more fully his reasons for the course of action he had taken. He had waited until Colt had grown into maturity and could feel satisfied that others in the family would approve of his being taken into the business as a safe pair of hands. Henry again expressed his fears:

> That he had seen for some time Past the Rapid progress of this Nations Ruin
> and could not tell how soon it might happen. It might be immediate but could
> not be far off – that the great National Debt must sooner or later be our Ruin.

Henry's overriding aim was to protect Stourhead. He did not want the estate, with its magnificent garden, to become an asset of the bank, and he could only avoid this outcome by severing all links between the property and the bank. He recognised that this would mean an irrevocable change of life for Colt, but he hoped that the gift of Stourhead, together with its estates, would more than recompense him. Colt had grown up spending time with Henry at Stourhead as a child; he'd seen the Temple of Apollo built and the Bristol Cross erected. They had a good relationship, and Henry knew that Colt would continue to care for his creation. He felt that this action would not be an injustice to Richard; Colt, after all, was his eldest son. He reminded Richard and Harry of Hester's small dowry and reiterated the necessity of including the Fleet Street premises, which would provide further income. His only wish now was to end his days '... at Clapham living on his Income from Business free from care and vexation'.

Harry now began to have some understanding of Henry's motives. But he was not convinced by his arguments. He wanted first to establish that Richard had not offended Henry at any time. Henry seemed taken aback by this suggestion and assured him that this was not the case.

Harry then began to lay out his counter-arguments, as he and his brother saw the situation. He first addressed the question of the house in Lincoln's Inn Fields, which Richard had understood would be given to him – and Henry confirmed that still was the intention. Harry then moved on to the more contentious issue of the bank premises. He asked Henry to confirm that the premises would be left to Richard, who was next in succession and would become Head of the Business on Henry's death. Henry was adamant that this was not his intention and that by leaving the Premises to Colt, Richard would become a tenant.

Harry now vehemently elaborated on his arguments. He pointed out that, should there be any differences of opinion in the future between Colt and the Partners, or their descendants, they could all be turned out of '... a House we had all been bred up in and spent our lives in by the caprice of any Person whatsoever and for what?'. Gaining momentum, he pointed out that the rent from Fleet Street was trifling and would not materially improve Colt's financial situation to any great extent. But he fervently pressed home his point, saying that Henry, by acting as he wished,

> ... might destroy the Happiness of a Family who had thro Life endeavoured to promote his to the utmost of their Power, might totally break up a Business that had for so many years been carried on with Reputation and Prosperity – that had enabled the Parties to increase their Substance so materially and he would ruin all this ... for about £100 per annum to Colt.

Henry was greatly shocked by the strength of these arguments. Far from meaning injustice to the family, he said, he meant them every benefit.

Reluctantly, he then agreed to leave the Fleet Street premises to Richard but remained adamant that Stourhead should go to Colt.

Harry and Richard were much relieved by the outcome. They asked, however, that Colt not be informed of the terms of the will too soon, nor that it should become general knowledge. They were afraid that, if the terms of the will came out before everything had been legally settled, it would 'alarm many whose Chief reason for Banking with us was, thinking the Property so Great, that Let what would happen, there could be no Loss to them on Account of the great assets'. Henry then agreed to pay Colt £1,000 per annum on the occasion of his marriage, to sign an irrevocable Private Deed to give Stourhead to Colt on his death and, by another irrevocable Private Deed, to secure to Richard his house in Lincoln's Inn Fields and the premises on Fleet Street on his death.

Richard Colt Hoare married Hester Lyttleton at Barnes in August 1783.

Henry retired to his house in Clapham.

The last gratuity paid to Francis was on 23rd October 1783. The ledger entry rather poignantly reads:

> By Francis Faugoin on settling his years acc. as usual.

Henry continued keeping accounts for the next two years, when living at Clapham. Entries in the ledger for 1785 detail payments from March to August, most of them to Ann Barugh, who was his housekeeper. A few years earlier, he had complained to Lord Ailesbury that he had rheumatism in his right hand and 'if it continues I must learn to write with my left hand if not too old to learn'. As he feared, his handwriting had deteriorated and become rather shaky, but the figures are as bold as ever. His indomitable spirit shows his utter determination to keep the habit of a lifetime – keeping meticulous accounts of his personal spending. The banker in him is not ready to give up yet.

The very last entry is on 25th August 1785. Unable to keep his hand steady, the writing slips away, trailing down the page. The effort required to pen those last few words and figures is palpable.

He died two weeks later, on 8th September 1785.

Sixteen years after Henry's death, visitors were still paying due respect and admiration to his vision. In 1801, a friend of Colt Hoare, John Britton, said:

> People of all ranks visited Stourhead … we cease to wonder at its national celebrity but it is the more to be admired from having been one of the first places laid out in the new style of gardening, and designed by a country gentleman, unassisted by any landscape gardener. Mr. Hoare, at an advanced age, had the heartfelt satisfaction to hear a place of his own creation universally admired, and to see a barren waste covered with the most luxuriant woods.[13]

His great friend, Coplestone Warre Bampfylde, also paid a moving tribute. He placed an urn in his garden at Hestercombe dedicated to his two closest friends, Henry Hoare and Charles Kemeys-Tynte. The inscription reads:

> Earth has not produced two such shining spirits as these
> Nor any with whom I have closer bonds.

It must have been hard for Francis to continue with the same enthusiasm. He'd spent most of his adult life working alongside Henry and had played his part in bringing to fruition Henry's vision. He'd been there through good times and bad. He must have taken some comfort, and perhaps a little pride, in what they had achieved together. Only three months after Henry's death, Francis lost the love of his life, Mary, who died on 8th December 1785. But life had to continue, and, like Henry, he had his grandchildren to give him pleasure. He retired from strenuous activities and went to live in a cottage on Bells Lawn on the estate. But he did continue to show visitors round the garden – who better to answer their questions?

The last mention of him is in an anonymous poem titled 'A Ride and a Walk through Stourhead'. One of the lines reads: '… weary Faugoine, silv'rd o'er by Care'.

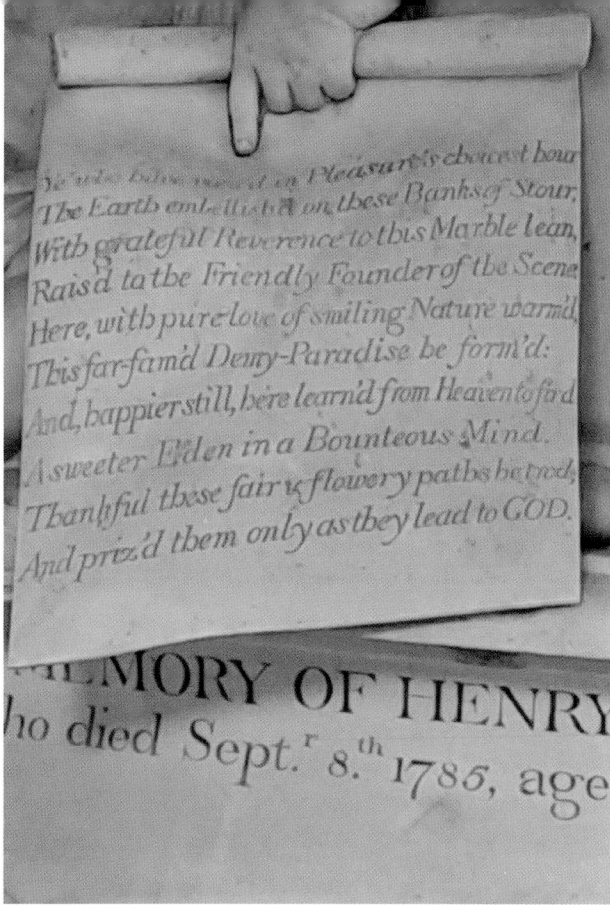

Henry Hoare II's memorial in church and close-up of scroll | Photograph: Alan Barker

Epitaphs to both Henry and Francis are in the church. On the chancel wall, a simple marble monument dedicated to Henry shows an urn and two putti holding a scroll, on which are engraved the following words.

Ye, who have view'd, in pleasure's choicest hour,
The earth embellish'd on the banks of Stour,
With grateful reverence to this marble lean,
Rais'd to the friendly founder of the scene.
Here with pure love of smiling nature warm'd,
This far-fam'd demi-paradise he form'd;
And happier still, here learn'd from Heaven to find
A sweeter Eden in a bounteous mind.
Thankful these fair and flowery paths he trod,
And prized them only as they led to God.

A 'far-fam'd demi-paradise' indeed.

The memorial to Francis is a marble tablet over one of the arches in the north aisle as you enter the church. This features a coat of arms and a motto which reads 'Vincit qui Patitur' – 'he who endures will succeed'. The names of the whole family follow:

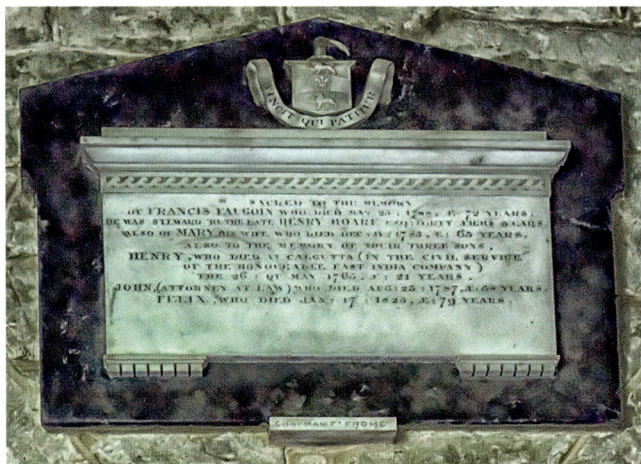

Faugoin family memorial in church
Photograph: Simon Newman

Sacred to the Memory of Francis Faugoin who died May 23 1788 age 72 years. He was steward to the late Henry Hoare Esq. Forty Eight Years. Also of Mary his wife who died Dec. 8 1785 aged 65 years. Also to the memory of their three sons. Henry who died in Calcutta (in the civil service of the Honourable East India Company) the 26 of May 1765 aged 21 years. John (Attorney at Law) who died Aug. 25 1787 aged 38 years. Felix who died Jan. 17 1825 aged 79 years.

I'm thankful there is this memorial to Francis in the church. It will remain in good condition and be legible for hundreds of years to come. The inscription on the tombstone is sadly already becoming harder to read and has deteriorated since I first noticed it all those years ago.

As I sit on the bench in the churchyard, close to Francis's tomb, and look across to where his house would have been, I think of him and of the journey I've taken to unravel his story. I think of all the people who have helped me along the way and those who have helped me to write this book. My hope is that Francis can now take his rightful place in the history of this special place: Francis Faugoin, Head Gardener at Stourhead.

1 Dodd, Dudley, ed. *The Letters of Henry Hoare 1760–1781.* Wiltshire Record Society, Wiltshire & Swindon History Centre, Chippenham, 2018. p. 156. WSA 1300/2950.

2 Ibid. WSA 1300/2881.

3 British Library, India Office Records: Ref. J/1/5 f.280.

4 Ibid.

5 Ibid.

6 Ibid.

7 Henry Faugoin will: Folio 42a of the Bengal Mayor's Court Proceedings 21/12/1763 to 20/12/1765. Shelf mark: IOR/P/154/52.

8 Letter Book. Press List of Public Department Records. Volume VIII, Press List Imperial Record Office 1770–1774, pp. 48 and 79. Shelf mark: IOR.354541.

9 Dodd, Dudley, ed. *The Letters of Henry Hoare 1760–1781.* Wiltshire Record Society, 2018. p. 155. WSA 1300/2944.

10 Ibid. p. 209. WSA 9/35/135 (2)2403.

11 Felix Faugoin will, 1825. The National Archives of the UK, Kew, Richmond, London TW9 4DU: PROB 11/1696/135.

12 Wiltshire & Swindon History Centre, Chippenham. Hoare archive: WSA 383/912.

13 Britton, John. The Beauties of Wiltshire. 1801.

CHAPTER SEVENTEEN

LEGACY

FROM THE BEGINNING, people have always visited Stourhead, and they still do. Friends meet up for a walk, followed by lunch, or tea and cake. Families bring their children and grandchildren to run and play and enjoy a picnic by the lake. Students come from all over the world to work, volunteer or just experience the reality of what they have previously only studied in books. Photographers love the light in the early evening; artists set up their easels and paint the trees and the temples. Some come alone, to experience the tranquillity of the place and maybe think about the loss of a loved one.

Henry always intended his garden to be used in this way. Visitors are enraptured by his pleasure grounds and they can mean all things to all people. Even if they don't know the meaning of the story, they can sense something deeper, the past pushing through the surface to the present. The beautiful scenes can trigger a deep emotional response and remain in the mind's eye for ever. The atmosphere is timeless, time before memory: it seeps into the soul.

My most memorable visits have been early in the morning, before visitors arrive, and in late afternoon, when the garden breathes a sigh of relief as the last visitors depart. As I stand, alone, looking across the lake, the garden is looking back at me. It feels as if I'm being drawn by an invisible force, calm and still and immutable. It's a powerful, physical and emotional feeling. And I know I'm not the only person to experience it.

I'm lucky enough to live only ten minutes away and to have witnessed the beauty of the seasons for many years. Winter brings drama to the landscape, especially on a cold, frosty day – and, even better, when it has snowed. Then a deep silence falls over the garden and the skeletal outline of the trees reveals their character. This is especially true of the sweet chestnuts on the drive. I almost like them better in the depths of winter; their twisted and gnarled shapes stand testament to their longevity. As I stand under Clock Arch, the first chestnut exudes a majestic presence, an awe-inspiring sight. I imagine him as a young sapling when Queen Elizabeth I was on the throne.

Early spring feels joyous: the intense green of young beech leaves, as they unfurl, contrasts with the equally intense blue of bluebells carpeting the ground beneath their feet. Birdsong fills the air; the fragrance of the yellow azaleas carries on the breeze and the meadow is filled with wild flowers.

It's often the ordinary walks that turn out to be special when you are least expecting it. One hot August day, I decided to walk from Clock Arch down the public road to the entrance to the garden. The road cuts a deep narrow cleft through the hillside and falls sharply away – a tunnel of cool, green shade giving a glimpse of light at the far end. Sunlight filters down through the tree canopy, throwing little pools of light onto the glossy green leaves of hart's tongue ferns growing on the steep banks each side of the road. These banks are clothed in a dense mat of vegetation: ferns, ivy, nettles, brambles, small specks of pink from herb robert and the odd wild rose. Hazel, holly and beech rise up through this mat of green, their branches joining together overhead, throwing a pattern of dappled shadows onto the road below. It's peaceful and calming. The speck of light beckons, and finally you emerge into the bright sunlight.

The sense of quiet calm is abruptly broken by the sight of crowds of people and buildings: to the left is the village hall, the Spread Eagle pub and the church, to the right, houses and cottages. Only then can you see the Bristol Cross coming into view. Nothing more is revealed at this point. If this were your first visit to Stourhead, you would have no inkling of what lies beyond the cross. Although this short walk is not part of the designed landscape, nor even beautiful – after all, it's down a public road – it epitomises so much about the quality and character of Stourhead. It illustrates the contrast between the simple and the dramatic, between open and closed spaces, between dark and light and all the little subtleties in between. When Henry was designing the garden, this is the effect he strove to achieve. He used his mind and imagination to create something that would last, that would endure and continue to give delight down the centuries.

When Henry made his first tentative steps towards making the garden, he chose to site the Temple of Ceres at the site of Paradise Well. Why was it called 'Paradise', long before this word was used to describe the garden? Maybe this spot was thought of as paradise and its special qualities recognised even then. The many springs bubbling up out of the ground were thought to be sacred – an entry point to another world. Henry was brought up on the classics at Westminster School, on Greek and Roman history, myths and legends. So, already he was using what became the hallmarks of the garden: water, architecture, the stories of the gods.

What is the spirit of this place? Much thought, time and discussion has been given over the years to the question 'What is the genius loci?'. For me, the question is easily answered.

The spirit of Stourhead is Henry the Magnificent. Henry's spirit is embedded in the garden; it's an extension of himself. His life's story is laid out before you. *Know my garden, know me.* Genius could be described as the ability to see what no one else has identified. Richard Colt Hoare recognised and acknowledged this when he said that Henry 'saw with his own eyes and suggested improvements with his own hands ...'. This is Henry's legacy. He poured everything he had into the creation of the garden: knowledge, love of art, energy and determination, and money.

If Henry has left such a powerful presence, where is Francis? Until now, his legacy has been unseen, but he is there, in the shadows, not far behind Henry. Or, perhaps, walking beside him discussing the next project. It's not difficult to imagine the expertise and care he poured into contributing his skill to bring Henry's ideas into being. The longevity of his employment speaks volumes for the relationship he forged with Henry and his family.

In my imagination, I feel Henry's presence most strongly when he's galloping on Miss Cade along Terrace Ride, relishing the exhilaration and enjoying the balmy breezes of a summer's morning. Francis I can see, early on that same summer morning, inspecting the crop of pineapples, testing for ripeness, his expert eye choosing which one to cut for the table that evening. An ordinary day in the lives of real people.

This, then, is *my* legacy: the discovery of the lives of these people, and the writing of this book. This is my labour of love and respect for those who have left us all such a beautiful place.

EPILOGUE

IT BEGAN WITH an ending. Maybe the ending of this story is just the beginning of another.

Maybe ten years from now, others will take up the challenge and answer the questions I haven't been able to answer. Maybe a hundred years from now, someone will discover this book in the Stourhead archives and be as fascinated by Francis Faugoin as I have been.

And maybe we can feel confident that, two hundred years from now, Stourhead will still be giving delight. And that the Hoare family will still be keeping a watchful eye on Henry the Magnificent's creation.

APPENDIX I

THE WOODEN
PALLADIAN BRIDGE

❧

ENRY THE MAGNIFICENT added features to his garden that do not exist today. Among them is the wooden Palladian bridge.

The bridge was a significant early feature in the garden. It served a practical purpose: providing the means of getting from one side of the valley to the other after the lake was formed. It was built in 1749, shortly after the Grotto and before the Pantheon. But, many years later, Colt Hoare removed it. He records in the Annals:

> In the summer 1798, I took down the Palladian Bridge, placed a ferry on the same spot.

Although this bridge became known as the 'Chinese' bridge, it was, in fact, a Palladian design. Palladio (1508–1580) was one of the most famous and influential architects of all time. His book, *I Quattro Libri dell'Architettura*, was translated into every major Western European language in the two centuries following its publication in 1570. Palladio looks back for his inspiration to the Roman architect of the Augustan age, Vitruvius, which would have resonated with Henry. Virgil, Horace and Ovid were all writers during the Augustan period and were studied by Henry and his contemporaries at Westminster School. The complete work of Palladio was translated into English by the architect, Isaac Ware, and published in 1738. Ware's patron, Richard Boyle, 3rd Earl of Burlington, suggested Ware make a faithful, exact copy of Palladio's work.

All the great and the good were subscribers to the Ware edition: His Grace the Duke of Montagu, the Right Honourable the Earl of Pembroke, the Honourable Charles Hamilton, Sir Robert Walpole, William Kent Esq., Mr William Hogarth, Mr Samuel Johnson and many other illustrious names, including Henry Flitcroft. Henry is not shown as being a subscriber, maybe because he was away on the Continent at the time of publication in 1738. He returned in 1741 and the bridge was completed circa 1749. As Henry chose two designs for bridges from this book (the other being the stone bridge), it's fair to assume that he did eventually own a copy.

Book III of Palladio's book describes streets, bridges and piazzas. Chapter V, 'Wooden Bridges', opens with the words:

> Bridges made of wood, either on one occasion only, like those which are made for all those accidents that usually happen in war; of which sort that is the most celebrated which Julius Caesar directed over the Rhine; or secondly, that they may perpetually serve the conveniency of everybody.

After this manner we read that Hercules built the first bridge that was ever made, over the Tiber, in the place where Rome was afterwards built.

We can only imagine the profound impact these words would have had on Henry. Was this the moment when the idea of Hercules, a Roman hero, became synonymous in his mind with his own Herculean efforts? And did he now decide to build another temple, dedicated to Hercules, bigger and more ambitious than the Temple of Ceres?

Palladio continues by describing a bridge over the River Cismone, a tributary of the Brenta, and gives clear instructions.

> The invention of this bridge is, in my opinion, very worthy of attention as it may serve upon all occasions … and because that bridges thus made are strong, beautiful and commodious. … The river where this bridge was ordered is one hundred foot wide; the breadth is divided into six equal parts; and at the end of each part (excepting the banks which are strengthened with pilasters of stone) the beams are placed that form the bed and breadth of the bridge.

This is almost exactly a description of the bridge built by Henry. Once again, it's not difficult to imagine him being inspired by these words, 'strong, beautiful, and commodious'. It was Vitruvius who said all buildings should display these three attributes – strength, utility and beauty – *firmitas*, *utilitas* and *venustas*. Henry was providing an aesthetic solution to a practical problem.

Palladio then went on to describe three more wooden bridges of a similar design, the last of which is the design chosen by Henry. Palladio says of this design: 'This last invention may be made with a greater or a smaller arch than it is here designed, according to the quality of the site, and as the greatness of the river shall require.'

We know that the bridge was an early feature. The Temple of Ceres was completed by 1745, and the Temple of the Nymph by 1748. The wooden Palladian bridge was in place by 1749, as shown by the entry in the ledger – 'in full for ye Bridge' – 'in full' signifying the final payment for work completed.

> Henry Hoare Ledger 1734–1749
> 4th December 1749.
> Mr Privett in full for ye Bridge & other work   £34 9s

As Privett was a stonemason, it is likely that he was responsible for building the foundations and abutments, but not for the wooden superstructure, which would have required the services of a carpenter. This may well have been Thomas Spinks, a craftsman Henry had used on previous occasions. At this date, no other bridges existed in the garden, because the lake had not yet been formed.

The building of the bridge shows that Henry had understood he could use the special advantages of the site. He knew that the presence of the medieval fishponds and the millpond indicated that the valley floor would hold water, due to the clay seam running underneath. He knew the river could be manipulated to create a much larger body of water, effectively flooding the valley and submerging these ponds. He also realised that, having created a lake, he would need a bridge from one side of the valley to the other.

Of course, being Henry, he also knew that this bridge would have to be a striking design. The bridge spanned the northern arm of the lake as it narrowed towards Six Wells valley, giving easy access from the west to the east bank. Built of oak and steeply arched, the distance spanned was approximately 100 ft. The design was unusual, both in the length of the bridge and the fact that it had a single, arching span, supported by stone abutments on each bank. The sides of the bridge were not closed in but had an open decorative design: a criss-cross pattern of timber struts. Open wooden steps led the visitor up onto the bridge, where it levelled out before descending again by open steps. Decorative stone urns were placed on each bank.

Why did the wooden Palladian bridge become known as 'Chinese'? Possibly because knowledge of China was just beginning to filter into the West at this point. Europe had begun importing Chinese ceramics and porcelain, and many of these pieces depicted scenes from gardens featuring arched bridges. All things Chinese were highly fashionable, and many wealthy aristocrats had Chinese lacquer cabinets in their houses. Coutts, the bankers, had Chinese wallpaper in their boardroom. Charles Hamilton's garden at Painshill had a so-called 'Chinese' bridge, and the Marchioness Grey's home at Wrest Park featured 'Chinoiserie', as it became known. Contemporary pattern books illustrated the delightful possibilities of enhancing your garden with Chinese features. John and William Halfpenny's pattern books in the Library at Stourhead show several different designs.[1]

Interpreting what was authentic was clearly a hit-and-miss affair. Most 'Chinese' garden features were anglicised and bore little resemblance to Chinese originals. It can only be assumed, therefore, that this fashion for Chinoiserie influenced visitors' perception of the design of the bridge – unless, of course, you were one of the cognoscenti.

There are many comments about the bridge from visitors. In 1762, Horace Walpole visited and noted: 'You pass over a wooden Palladian Bridge with Urns.'[2] We can be sure he would not have mistaken its provenance.

Sixteen years after it was first built, a letter dated 1765 from an unknown female reads: 'We then walked over the Chinese Bridge which is excessive pretty, it consists of one large Arch, it is boarded all over and assends by steps at each end.' This letter was given to the National Trust in 2004 by Mrs Janet Ede of Norwich. She found it when clearing the belongings of a relation who had passed away, but she had no idea who had written it.

So, by 1765 it was being referred to as 'Chinese'.

In 1770, Bampfylde drew a panoramic pencil sketch of the west side of the lake. This clearly shows a single-span, steeply arched bridge with decorative urns placed at each end.[3] He also drew a charming little sketch showing people in a rowing boat about to pass under the bridge.

Six years later, when Mrs Lybbe Powys visited in 1776, she was thoroughly confused:

> We then passed over what the gardener called a Palladian Bridge,
> but he certainly mistook, as I think Palladio's bridges were cover'd over.
> This is open top and sides, pretty at a distance; when near, the idea of going over
> a kind of ladder only is frightful. Another party of company could not bring
> themselves to venture, but 'tis not so bad after you have brought yourself to
> venture a few of its steps, tho' its perpendicular appearance and seeing the water
> through at first looks formidable.[4]

So, the gardener who showed Mrs. Powys round – clearly Francis – did not make a mistake.

Visitors from Europe gave an even more detailed description of the bridge. Fredrik Magnus Piper (1746–1824) was a Swedish architect employed by King Gustav III. In 1774, the King awarded him a grant to study 'modern English landscape gardening'. He came to England in 1779 for a second time, on this occasion visiting Stowe and Stourhead.

Piper was clearly enchanted by the garden. In his book *Description of the Idea and General Plan for an English Park*, written in 1811–1812, he describes:

> ... what I believe should be noted during journeys in England at the most
> extensive and most costly of all the Park constructions built in that country at
> Stowe ... This Park contains an unusual number of ornaments of a dimension,
> size and multiplicity which betrays a desire to win renown and precedence
> before all others, with respect to both cost and size, but which has, for that
> reason, lost much of the simple and rustic reputation and the Romantic and
> picturesque Character which one experiences with such great delight in the
> previously mentioned Park at Stourton.

'Simple and rustic' and 'Romantic and picturesque', giving 'great delight' when compared with the grandeur of Stowe. These are all the attributes that captivated philanthropist Jonas Hanway when he visited – and that still charm us today. As Hanway wrote, 'All is grand or simple, or a beautiful mixture of both.'

Piper drew a plan of the lake and its environs, showing the location of all the features in the garden, together with a key. The plan also showed a drawing of the bridge in the top left-hand corner. Further detailed architectural drawings gave cross-sections of the handrails, the foundations and exact measurements and spacing required for the steps.[5] Small photographic copies of the original plans are held at the V&A.[6] Further copies can be found in the Research Room at Stourhead.[7]

These drawings also show details of the decorative urns placed on pedestals, located at each end of the bridge. They were carved by the Bath stone-mason Robert Parsons (1718–1790). The 1749–1770 Henry Hoare ledger gives details of payments to Parsons from 14th April 1750 to 18th September 1761, totalling £190. 85 s.

Another visitor to the garden was a French amateur artist, Lancelot Henri Roland Turpin de Crissé (1754–c.1800). He fled to England with his wife and two children to escape the French Revolution. He visited Stourhead in 1793 and made drawings of the bridge. His sketchbook is held at the Museum of Fine Art, Angers, Maine et Loire, France.

The Turpin de Crissé drawing gives more detailed information about the appearance, the urns and the criss-cross design of the handrails. It also shows the presence of a fence in the same design as the handrails, extending from the bridge and curving away into the garden. All these drawings and visitor comments show how much the bridge was admired. As with the Grotto, visitors experienced a little frisson of fear and anxiety when crossing over, looking down through open steps to the water below.

There was another reason for building the bridge. At this date, there was no footpath between the first and second pond at the head of the valley. This first pond is now known as Lily Lake and the second, Diana's Basin. It is likely a rough path may have been in existence, but it could have been overgrown with trees and would certainly have been very wet, as it's level with Lily Lake – a continuing problem today. Henry wished to position the bridge so that it hid the exact extent of the main lake, giving the impression that it goes on beyond the bridge. The lake narrows at this point and becomes more river-like, curving away into the distance. Today, the trees lining the bank dip down to the water, and as the 'river' gently meanders, it forms a little shallow bay on the east bank, before disappearing out of sight. Henry wished to disguise the boundaries of the lake because the original design intention was to ensure that the route would be contained within the garden, keeping the attention of the visitor focused on the garden itself. Henry wished to maintain an illusion of a 'perfect paradise' without any distractions from the outside world, a sense of a magical, enclosed space, an almost dream-like immersion in the landscape. Even today the garden still has this indefinable quality.

Henry was an admirer of Alexander Pope and probably knew very well his *Epistle to Lord Burlington*, first published in 1731, as he quoted from it in his letters. Pope continued to revise this poem; in the final publication of his collected works, in 1744, shortly before Pope's death, the poem is entitled *Epistles to Several Persons: Epistle IV*. The poem provides a template perfectly illustrated by the design of the garden: 'surprise, variety and concealment'.

> Let not each beauty ev'rywhere be spied,
> Where half the skill is decently to hide.
> He gains all points, who pleasingly confounds,
> Surprises, varies, and conceals the bounds.

Henry's skill was to achieve these instructions, taking them off the page and into his garden. And Francis helped him to turn them into reality, a feat of ingenuity and imagination that still surprises and pleases us today.

1   Halfpenny, William and Halfpenny, John. *New Designs for Chinese Bridges, Temples, Triumphal Arches, Part II.* 1752.

2   Walpole, Horace. *Journal of Visits to Country Seats &c.* Volume XVI. Ed. Paget Toynbee. The Walpole Society, Oxford. 1927–8.

3   Prints and Drawings Room at the V&A: E360-1949 WD 110A.

4   Climenson, Emily J., ed. *Passages from the Diaries of Mrs. Philip Lybbe Powys of Hardwick House, Oxon, 1756–1808.* Longmans, London, 1889.

5   Royal Swedish Academy of Fine Arts in Stockholm.

6   V&A Crypt Store. General Collection: Pressmark A.96 Box 1 Barcode 634675.

7   Stourhead Research Room Catalogue No. B4.16.

APPENDIX II
PARADISE 'LOST'

T HE PALLADIAN BRIDGE was not the only feature in Henry's garden that his grandson, Richard Colt Hoare, removed. We know that there were many others. Henry has been quoted as saying, 'I lived to see a desert converted into a Paradise', a reference maybe to Milton's poem, *Paradise Lost*. We also know that Henry had been introduced to the poems of Milton by William Benson, his brother-in-law. I thought it appropriate, therefore, to refer to the features that Richard Colt Hoare removed as 'lost' from 'Paradise', and 'lost' to us today.

The Turkish Tent and the Hermitage are well known, but the Gothic Greenhouse and others were a little harder to track down. When I first heard of the existence of these features, I was intrigued and determined to discover more about them. Once again, my curiosity took me down unexpected paths.

A good way of getting to know these features is to follow in Henry's footsteps as he conducted friends around the garden. Unusually, the garden cannot be seen from the house. Originally, there was a double flight of steps on the south front of the house; when walking down these steps and across the south lawn, there is nothing to indicate a garden in the valley below. The first realisation that the ground falls sharply away is the unexpected view down the hillside onto the roof of a church. The path leads on through trees until suddenly, the Temple of Apollo comes into view across the valley. This must have been as much of a 'wow' moment for Henry's visitors as it is for visitors today.

But Henry's visitors had many more delights to come.

The first feature to claim attention was the Temple on the Terrace, originally called the Venetian Seat. This was a small, classically inspired building, located to the left of what is now known as Apollo View and close to the start of the Fir Walk.

In 2003, when thinning the laurels in this area, the garden team discovered the foundations. Richard Higgs, the Head Gardener at the time, invited the Regional Archaeologist, Martin Papworth, to examine the footings of the building they had uncovered. Martin then conducted a detailed excavation of the site and prepared a report.[1] He concluded that 'from the evidence it appears the building footings lie near the mapped position of the mid-18th century Temple on the Terrace as drawn by Piper in 1779 and demolished at the end of the 18th century by Richard Colt Hoare'.

The report stated:

> ... it seems almost certain that the Temple faced west towards the landscape garden. ... and on the east side was a blank wall which backed onto woodland. An overgrown pathway leading up the steep south slope to reach the terrace in front of the building may also be contemporary with the temple construction.

It also stated that the Piper plan showed the upper terrace '... leading from Stourhead house and the statue of Apollo Belvedere to the Temple on the Terrace. On the north side ... the route divides, with the main terrace turning north and continuing to the Obelisk.'

Helpfully, Fredrik Piper made a drawing of this temple. It shows an open-fronted building; four Doric pillars supported a deep architrave, or lintel, broken by a semi-circular arch. On each side of this arch, a round niche contained a female bust, and a carved female head occupied the position of the keystone. Low balustrades acted as in-fill between the pillars. The whole was finished off by a classical triangular pediment.

Why did Henry place a temple in this location, facing the valley, long before the lake and other features were in place? We can't be sure: was it an early experiment with a designed walk – passing the statue of Apollo en route to the Temple on the Terrace, then turning right along the Fir Walk to the Obelisk? And why did Colt Hoare remove a building which was of a classical design?

Later, a Coade stone copy of the Borghese Vase was placed in the Temple.

The Borghese Vase was a large, bell-shaped vessel used in ancient Greece for diluting wine with water, placed in the centre of the room at banquets. It was made of marble, with carved figures depicting a procession of revellers following Bacchus, the god of wine. The vase was rediscovered in a Roman garden in 1566 and was acquired by the noble Italian family Borghese. Today, it is in the Louvre.

In 1769, Mrs Eleanor Coade bought Daniel Pincot's struggling artificial stone business at King's Arms Stairs, Lambeth, London. This business developed into Coade's Artificial Stone Manufactory, with, unusually for the time, Eleanor in charge of the whole operation. She ran this successful business until her death in 1821. The artificial stone was manufactured to a secret recipe and took great skill to produce. Using moulds, Coade stone was ideal for producing large statues and decorative objects and was highly resistant to weathering. When Colt Hoare removed the temple, he placed the Coade stone vase in the Temple of Flora, where it still stands today.

An exact copy of this temple was placed in the garden at Dessau-Wörlitz. This famous German garden lies between Dessau and Wörlitz, south-west of Berlin. It was the creation of Prince Friedrich Franz of Anhalt-Dessau and his friend Baron von Erdmannsdorf. They came to England in 1764 and visited numerous gardens, including Stourhead. The impressions and experiences Prince Friedrich Franz gained in England became guiding lights for his future life as a prince of the Enlightenment. It was then that he first developed his love of landscape gardens, and Erdmannsdorf a love of architecture. Determined to create a garden based on what they had seen in England, they returned home and chose Wörlitz as a starting point. The first feature to be built was an exact copy of the Venetian Seat at Stourhead, which they named the English Seat.

Anne and I were keen to visit this garden and see what this feature, missing from Stourhead, would have looked like; although a copy, it was an 18th-century copy.

The garden is set on the flood-plain of the River Elbe, close to the small town of Wörlitz. Many waterways criss-cross the extensive site, offering the opportunity of boat trips. We took a trip on one of these boats, which provided the chance of viewing the garden from the water. There's a Temple of Flora, a Gothic House – modelled on Strawberry Hill – a Temple of Venus, a Pantheon, and many more buildings, bridges, and statues. As we entered the Temple of the Night, through a dark passageway, the ghostly white figure of a Vestal Virgin suddenly appeared, as if floating in mid-air. It was quite a physical shock and brought home to me the emotions felt by visitors when entering the Grotto at Stourhead. Another ingenious feature in this garden was a representation of Mount Vesuvius. This enormous undertaking was a tour-de-force, which spouted real flames, smoke and larva flow. This spectacular sight can still be seen on special occasions, these days using modern technology for dramatic effect.

There was so much to see; it took three days to explore the site. We stayed within walking distance of the garden, and entry was free. A highlight was an unexpected and memorable encounter with a German family. While queuing for a coffee, the woman in front of us asked why we were visiting – in, I hasten to add, impeccable English. When we explained that we worked at Stourhead and had come to see this famous copy, she immediately invited us to join her family and meet her husband. He was astounded and delighted to meet us, bombarding us with many questions about Stourhead. We were equally astounded when he pulled a book from his rucksack. There, on the front, was the iconic view of the Pantheon across the lake. It turned out he was an architect living in Berlin and had long wanted to visit Stourhead. It was a reminder to both of us that so many people think of Stourhead as a special place.

Returning to Stourhead: after the Temple on the Terrace, the next thing to see on the visitors' tour was a small round seat named the Chinese Umbrella. Located at Apollo View, Fredrik Piper also made a sketch of this little feature. Shaded by the 'umbrella', it provided the chance to sit and take in the view. Today, a long, curved bench provides the same opportunity.

Continuing along the path, the next perfect little cameo appears on the left. This is my favourite view of the Pantheon: framed by the trees and reflected in the lake, it seems to be suspended over the water. Enchanting as this view is – and visitors always linger a long time in complete silence – we continue straight ahead along the edge of the valley.

The next surprise was truly magnificent. Placed on a mound, a huge Turkish tent looked directly down the hillside to the wooden Palladian bridge and across the lake to the Pantheon. It could, itself, be seen from both these features. Today, the hillside is covered with trees, but when climbing up the hill from the wooden Palladian bridge in Henry's day, visitors approached the tent by a zig-zag path that crossed an open area of smooth grass.

This prominent position is depicted on a 952-piece dinner service called the Green Frog Service – which is the only representation of the tent we have. The Green Frog Service was commissioned by Catherine the Great of Russia in 1773. It was made by Josiah Wedgwood, and every piece had a hand-painted view of English landscape gardens. It was intended for a new summer palace built on marshy ground some miles from St. Petersburg. The palace acquired the name of La Grenouillère (or, the Frogpond) – hence the inclusion of a green frog motif on every piece.

There are several written references to the tent. Richard Colt Hoare noted in the Annals:

> January 1792 Levelled the hill on which the Turkish Tent formerly stood.

And:

> 1832 Thinned the old Turkish Tent hill.

The unknown female visitor mentioned earlier wrote a detailed description on 10th August 1765:

> ... we next walked to the Turkish Tent, a very pretty Invention. It is Covered with white Linnen and fringed with Blue, the inside is Painted Blue & White in Stripes like a Sattinn, there is three half Moons on the Top which you see at a great distance ...

Eleven years later, Henry took advice from his daughter, Susanna, on the appearance of the design of the interior and altered it in accordance with her wishes, referred to in a letter to his grand-daughter Harriot, dated 18th July 1776:

> ... Bless Her for the improvements She made whilst here & the inside of
> The Tent is alterd as She directed looks sweetly & much admired...[2]

Mrs Lybbe Powys visited in 1779, and said:

> The Turkish Tent at Mr. Hoare's is very pretty; 'tis of painted canvas, so remains up the whole year; the inside painted blue and white in mosaic.

It must have been an exotic sight. It was a large structure, open at the front, with seating for several people. The bright blue and white design topped with three gold crescents would have stood out against the backdrop of green trees, especially when viewed across the lake from the Pantheon.

Charles Hamilton erected a Turkish Tent at Painshill in 1759, probably taken from a design by the architect, Henry Keene, in 1755. Henry visited Painshill sometime before 1762, and it is almost certain he copied this idea. There was friendly rivalry between Henry and Hamilton.

Not everyone admired the tent. When Parnell visited Stourhead he commented, 'On the bank opposite the Attic Temple [the Pantheon] is a Turkish tent taken from Mr. Hamiltons, very elegant but rather inferior to his.'

It was still causing comment after Henry's death. When the novelist Fanny Burney's half-sister, Maria Rishton, wrote to Fanny in 1786, she described her visit to Stourhead and mentioned 'a beautiful Turkish Tent such as Sultans take out when they go to war'.

Knowledge of these tents filtered into Europe after the Siege of Vienna. The Holy Alliance defeated the Ottoman army at the Battle of Vienna on 14th September 1683, stopping the advance of the Ottoman Empire into Europe. The army fled the battlefield, leaving behind their campaign tents, which were seized as booty of war. The largest collection of tents is in the Krakow National Museum in Poland; examples also exist in the gardens of Haga Royal Park in Stockholm, Sweden. Once again, anglicised examples became the latest fashionable 'must have' and appeared at Vauxhall Gardens in London and in landscape gardens around the country.

We now have to retrace our steps back to the point where the path begins its zig-zag descent to the lake. The Chinese Alcove was located at a hairpin bend on the path, facing not over the lake, but back towards the Temple of Flora and the village. There are no representations of this feature, but the location is shown quite clearly on the Piper plan. The plan shows a square structure with, perhaps, steps at the entrance.

I knew there was an example of a Chinese pavilion at Wrest Park in Bedfordshire, the home of the Marchioness de Grey. Once again, I stayed with my sister, Vicky, in Northamptonshire and we visited shortly after the garden opened to the public, following its restoration by English Heritage.

The Wrest Chinese Pavilion is a small, square building, made of wood and open at the sides with steps up to the entrance. The roof is shaped like a pagoda, with bells hanging from each corner, and a golden dragon placed on top. It is white, with a red geometric design painted on panels inside and outside the building. It is a charming little feature and must have been a delightful stopping-place to sit and chat with friends. As the ground plan is the same as the one shown on the Piper plan, I think this must be a close approximation of the feature at Stourhead.

Henry's brother, Sir Richard, was also following fashion and erecting a Chinese pavilion in his garden at Barn Elms in Surrey. In May 1752, accounts refer to 'making a scaffold in & around the Chinese temple for the use of Mr. Harden painter', and two weeks later for 'fixing the dragon on the Temple'.[3]

Chinese pavilions were extremely popular. The Chinese House at Stowe is a highly decorative example, with panels depicting figures and flowers. One at Shugborough was featured on the Green Frog Service. Francis would have been familiar with this fashion, as Duke John had a fine example, which can still be seen at Boughton House. It was commissioned by the duke in 1745 and could be dismantled and taken inside for winter storage. Dragons were painted on the underside of the roof, with the obligatory dragon sitting on the top. Perhaps there was a smaller version at Ditton?

Leaving the influence of China behind, Henry then showed his visitors the last feature on this hillside. The Gothic Greenhouse was set on the original path running behind the Temple of Flora. It faced down the hillside, with a sightline to the stone

Turkish Tent, Painshill | Photograph: the author

The Pavilion, Wrest Park | Photograph: the author

Palladian bridge and the Temple of Apollo. On the Piper plan, there appears to be a wide, smooth approach across a small amphitheatre of grass, precisely the same as the approach to the Turkish Tent. This meant that both features could clearly be seen from the opposite side of the lake.

So, when taking the route from the house and walking down the hillside, the Gothic Greenhouse was the last feature to be seen. When entering the garden at the Bristol Cross, it was the first. This is corroborated by comments from our friend the unknown female visitor, Sir John Parnell and Mrs Lybbe Powys.

> 1765 (unknown visitor) The first I saw was a Green House, the inside and roof was lined with little pebbles, looked very pretty.

> 1768 (Sir John Parnell) On entering the grounds by this cross are two or three pretty cottages neatly ornamented with trees but thatched which I much admire for its simplicity. Soon after you pass thro a winding shrubbery and meet a small Gothic green-house built of coarse flints, with Gothic pilasters.

> 1776 (Mrs Lybbe Powys) The next building after the Cross is a greenhouse, prettily adorn'd outside by stone or burnt cinders from the glass-houses at Bristol, the inside black gravel stone mixed in the mortar; it looks like pounded flints and has a pretty effect.

Horace Walpole gives a brief reference in 1762 in 'Visits to Country Seats'. He is rather dismissive, noting 'a greenhouse of false Gothic'. The term 'greenhouse' had a different meaning from the one we use today. It referred to a building used to protect 'greens' from winter weather, which usually meant tender plants such as orange trees. Very often, these buildings were also called Orangeries. Fredrik Piper used the term 'Orangery' in the key to his plan.

Were there ever any greens or orange trees? When the Piper plan is closely examined, it's possible to see what might be interpreted as potted plants lining each side of the approach. This would make sense: many examples of orange trees in large terracotta pots can be seen as a decorative element in Italian gardens. For Henry and his contemporaries, they would have been a fashionable Italianate touch. However, this is just a theory, and sadly we will never know.

A small, tantalisingly faint outline of the Gothic Greenhouse can just be seen in a panorama of the east side of the lake, drawn by Bampfylde. Sections of this panorama are shown in the National Trust Guidebook of 2002. I knew this pencil sketch was included in a large portfolio of his work held in the Prints and Drawings room at the V&A,[4] so there was nothing to be done but to go and see the original to try to discover more detail; Anne was just as keen to come with me.

The portfolio turned out to be a large volume, full of interesting sketches. The panorama was drawn on a long piece of paper folded into the volume. As we slowly and carefully unfolded the paper, we could see the wooden Palladian bridge, the Temple of Flora hidden among the trees, and there, right on the edge of the paper, the Gothic Greenhouse. I have to admit to letting out a gasp of delight in the hallowed silence of the Prints and Drawings room.

Exactly as I hoped, Bampfylde's sketch showed far more detail. The building had the typical Gothic design of three ogee arches, surmounted by a fretted, or pierced, frieze and decorative pinnacles. Once again, an open front had seating in the interior, which allowed a view of the stone bridge and Apollo. At Painshill, an octagonal building, painted white and made of wood, has similar features. The Gothic Exedra at Painswick in Gloucestershire looks even more like Bampfylde's drawing; this is also made of wood but is not three-dimensional.

What was the building material referred to by Mrs. Powys? What exactly did she mean when she said, 'prettily adorned outside by stone or burnt cinders from the glasshouses at Bristol'?

It's known that Henry quarried stone from around the perimeter of the garden. He commented, 'I have ransacked the bowels of the earth for building stone.' The remains of a quarry can be seen along the track from the Temple of Apollo to Clock Arch. This track gave access to carts and wagons moving stone and building materials used in the construction of Apollo. Indeed, Apollo sits on a plateau which was created as a result of this quarrying activity. The stone quarried was chert, a hard rock that resists erosion and is similar to flint. Along this track is the one place where chert can be seen in situ; it sits in layers between the greensand. The lower surface of chert is smooth, black, and shiny, and the top pitted. Mrs. Powys was trying to describe a material she had not seen before and I think, in this case, she did a good job.

To enable the construction of the fine detailing of ogee arches and pinnacles, freestone would have had to be used. The ogee arch was a popular Gothic design, which imitated medieval cathedral windows. The Convent has a similar design, having walls of rough lumps of stone and window frames made of smooth freestone. Freestone is a stone used in masonry and is so named because it can be freely cut in any direction without shattering or splitting. I found this feature the most satisfying to research: so little was known about it, proving my research to be quite a challenge.

All these features – the Temple on the Terrace, the Turkish Tent, the Chinese Alcove and the Gothic Greenhouse – caused comment and gave enjoyment by their variety and ingenuity. They also provided places to sit and admire the view; to discuss the design of the garden or the burning questions of the day; or to just sit and chat while sheltering from unexpected showers. What a pity they are no longer there. Visitors today are provided with only unimaginative wooden benches.

Sir John Parnell wrote the most detailed account of the garden I have yet found, and is the only visitor to mention a particularly entertaining feature. Located on the path somewhere close to the entrance to Rock Arch:

> Here stands, level almost with the surface of the lake, a kind of seat which, tho'
> no ornament in itself, is the best contrived seat I know to take in the ornaments
> of a fine situation, as by moving your foot you can take in a new portion of the
> scene when you have sufficiently examined another. It is formd of a great butt
> or porter hogshead cut in the front and a seat fixd in with the top sloped up to
> keep off the weather. It is prettiest painted all green, except the top which may
> be slate colour... It rests on a pivot below and with a foot may be turned as the
> person sitting in it pleases. They say Queen Elizabeth was the first inventor of
> these and built one at Ham.

He then accompanied this comment with a little sketch showing the barrel converted to a seat with a little conical 'hat'. I am sure children today would love to spin round in such an amusing object.

The last 'lost' feature was the Hermitage. It was a late addition to the garden, being put together in 1771 and completed in 1772. Parson Woodforde refers to it in his diary:

> 2nd June 1772 The Hermitage at Mr. Hoare's by the Temple of Apollo is very
> pretty indeed and quite new, began last Christmas.

Henry took advice on the location from Charles Hamilton, who suggested blocking the old, direct route up the hill to Apollo, and creating a new zig-zag path which passed directly through the Hermitage en route to the temple – exactly the same design as walking through the Grotto en route to the Pantheon.

Fredrik Piper drew several detailed sketches showing the Hermitage in plan and elevation, as well as further sketches of the entrance and interior. These drawings show the same ground plan as the Grotto, with a winding entrance passageway and exit. Upturned tree trunks with exposed roots formed the arch-like entrance. The passage opened into a central chamber with an apex roof that increased the ceiling height. A shaft of light from an opening in the roof fell onto a table with an hourglass and old bones. A hanging lamp completed the picture and a chamber to the rear was presumably a sleeping area.

Hermits were hugely popular in 18th-century gardens. They were seen as 'natural' specimens of humanity. Wealthy landowners would even hire hermits to occupy their hermitages, which were usually sited in woods, overlooking water, and constructed of natural materials. Owls, signifying wisdom, perched on the roof and the hourglass and human bones symbolised the passing of time and mortality: the sands of time running out and the inevitability of death.

Henry, it seems, did not hire a resident hermit. He had other ideas. The great pleasure and sense of fun he felt when designing and building this feature leap out of this letter to Harriot:

> *30th November 1771*
> I am building a Hermitage above the Rock & when you are about a Quarter part up the walk from the Rock to The Temple of Apollo you turn short to the right & so zigzag up to it & thence go under The Trees to The Temple of Apollo as M^r. Hamilton advised & We stop or plant up in Clumps the old Walk up the Hill to that Temple. It is to be lined inside and out with Old Gouty nobby oakes the Bark on which M^r. Grove & my Neighbours are so kind to give me & Mr. Chapman a Clergyman show'd me one yesterday called Judge Wyndham's seat which I taken to be the year of our Lord 1,000 and I am [quite (*inserted*)] sure it is not ante Diluvian. I believe I shall put in to be myself The Hermit.[5]

I am sure Harriot would have been highly amused by that comment. Perhaps the idea of being a hermit appealed to Henry. From time to time, we all dream of being released from the stresses and pressures of daily life to live in idyllic surroundings.

This letter refers to Judge Wyndham's seat, shown to Henry by the Rev. John Chapman MA. Chapman was the vicar of Silton Church in the hamlet of Silton, a few miles from Stourton. An enormous memorial sculpture by Jan van Nost dominates the small church, in memory of Sir Hugh Wyndham, a famous resident of the parish. He was appointed Judge of the Court of Common Pleas in 1654 by Oliver Cromwell. After being imprisoned in the Tower at the Restoration, he was pardoned and knighted by Charles II. Sir Hugh bought the Manor of Silton in 1641, and the ancient oak tree in a nearby field became a favourite resting place from which to admire the view over the Royal Forest of Gillingham. It was said to be the site of hangings after the Monmouth Rebellion of 1685. The Wyndham oak, as it became known, was so famous it was the subject of an engraving during the reign of George III. More recently, it was included in a worldwide series of photographs, all taken at the dawn of the new millennium.

The Wyndham oak was an ancient tree when Sir Hugh bought the Manor in 1641 and, as Henry said, reputed to be 1,000 years old. Amazingly, this tree is still alive and (fairly) well, in a field behind the church. It's an astonishing sight, completely hollow in the centre with a huge swollen and distorted girth. Touching a tree which has seen so many centuries of history is a sobering experience. It's wonderful to think that this tree was the inspiration and model for Henry's Hermitage.

So, the 'paradise' of Henry's original garden, as he envisaged it, is lost to us today. Some of these features remained in place for more than thirty years, but Richard Colt Hoare eventually removed them all. He didn't dismantle the Hermitage until 1814, forty-three years after it was built.

Why did Colt Hoare take away these features, so exotic and intriguing – and offering so much more varied a vision than the essentially neo-classical landscape we see today? There are several reasons. Eclectic collections of exotic garden features were already going out of fashion by the time he inherited Stourhead. In addition, Colt Hoare actively disapproved of them. An acquaintance, John Britton, asked Colt Hoare to write a dedication to his book *The Beauties of Wiltshire* but Colt Hoare took him to task by saying:

> You have totally mistaken the character intended to have been given to the lake and its environs. It was intended by Henry Hoare the second – who had travelled a good deal abroad – to give these grounds the character of an Italian villa, with a lake surrounded by temples etc. and in this he succeeded partly and would have done so totally had he not admitted those which were incongruous in their taste and which I have taken down. I shall, therefore, substitute the following description as more accurate:

> At the period when these gardens were laid out it was the fashion in England to overcrowd the ground with buildings (as at Stowe and Stourhead) and we remember to have seen Chinese and Turkish buildings admitted amongst those of a purer Grecian taste. All of these have been judiciously removed by the present proprietor and thus the buildings which decorate these gardens are rendered uniform in their taste and style.

Colt Hoare wished to restore the gardens to what he perceived to be Henry's original idea. That word of his – 'purer' – is revealing. But the Temple on the Terrace was a classical design, so why did he remove this? Colt Hoare was a reserved character and may well have been sensitive to criticism.

The poet and satirist, Richard Graves (1715–1804) lived at Claverton, near Bath, and moved in the outer circle of Henry's associates. He penned a satirical novel, *Columella*, describing three friends, Atticus, Hortensius and Columella, visiting Stourhead where they poked fun at the varied collection of garden features. Bampfylde designed the frontispiece for this, published in 1779.[6]

> When the three gentlemen arrived at Stourhead, Atticus and Hortensius were seized with the utmost rapture at the beauty of the valley ... After they had examined the scene however ... and began to observe objects more attentively, Atticus took the liberty ... to criticise the modern taste of jumbling together so many buildings of such a different style of architecture and of ages and nations so remote from each other.

On a more practical note, most of these features were built from ephemeral materials which would not have stood the test of time and perhaps had begun to look shabby.

Colt Hoare was a different character from his extrovert, sociable grandfather. His interests included the new discipline of archaeology: he was one of the first people to assist in excavating at Stonehenge by funding the antiquarian William Cunnington; he was a historian, writing a *History of Ancient Wiltshire*; he was also a respected botanist, being invited to become a member of the Linnaean Society; his collection of pelargoniums was acknowledged to be the finest in the country. All these subjects required obsessive attention to detail. He did, however, share a love of art with his grandfather and, unlike him, was an accomplished artist himself.

Although Colt Hoare changed the original design, he dearly loved his grandfather and continued to care for the garden. It's thanks to him we have the diary, or Annals, of the improvements he made, which he kept so meticulously and urged others to 'do likewise'.

He also quoted his grandfather, saying:

> I have heard him say that he never thought seriously of enriching his grounds
> by plantations, until he had attained the age of forty years; but when he once
> began, he proceeded, *con spirito*, upon a widely extended scale, covering a
> barren waste with wood; and happily lived to see the good effects of his designs,
> and to enjoy the gratifying sight of a desert converted into a paradise; in short,
> he acted from the most liberal motives and adopted in all his actions this motto,
> Non sibi, sed posteris.

Non sibi, sed posteris. Not for ourselves but for those who come after. I think we can truly say that 'those who come after' have all continued to care for his creation. Today, the National Trust's mantra is 'For everyone, for ever'. Henry would have approved.

1   Papworth, Martin. *Temple on the Terrace. Archaeological Excavation. Stourhead Landscape Garden.* National Trust, July 2003. NT SMR No. 114077: ST7754 3405.

2   Dodd, Dudley, ed. *The Letters of Henry Hoare 1760–1781.* Wiltshire Record Society, Wiltshire & Swindon History Centre, Chippenham, 2018. Vol. 71, p. 163. WSA 1300/2947.

3   Miller, Sally. *Garden History Journal*, Vol. 38, p. 194.

4   V&A Prints and Drawings Room. Sketch with Grotto, Wooden Bridge, Obelisk, Temple of Flora, Gothic Greenhouse, Stone Bridge: E387. 1949. Folio 92.D.62.

5   Dodd, Dudley, ed. *The Letters of Henry Hoare 1760–1781.* p. 132. WSA 9/35/165(2)/1478.

6   Turner, James. 'The Chinese Alcove at Stourhead. A Contemporary Sneer', *Journal of Garden History*, Vol. 7, No. 2, Summer 1979. pp. 102–104.

INDEX

*References in **bold** are to images*